Michael Tippett was born on 2 January 1905 in London, but spent most of his childhood in Suffolk and later in the South of France and Italy. He studied composition and conducting at the Royal College of Music. After graduating he taught French for a few years before retiring to live very simply in a small village in Surrey. His early years during the Depression were fraught with difficulties and it was not until 1935 that he felt he had found his style and perfected his technique. The war was a testing time: in 1940 he was appointed Musical Director of Morley College just after its facilities had been blitzed; in 1943 his pacifist convictions resulted in a three-month prison sentence. His war-time oratorio, *A Child Of Our Time*, revealed his special gift for the expression of deep collective feeling.

Since then his creative output has won him international recognition. His visionary opera, *The Midsummer Marriage*, was produced at Covent Garden in 1955 and its opulence ran through a whole sequence of instrumental works. His musical development evolved still further with his second opera, the tragic *King Priam*, and his third opera, *The Knot Garden*, was rapturously received at Covent Garden in 1970. In addition he has composed three symphonies and many instrumental and choral works. Sir Michael was knighted in 1966.

Moving

Sir Michael Tippett

into Aquarius

Paladin

Granada Publishing Limited
Published in 1974 by Paladin Books
Frogmore, St Albans, Herts AL2 2NF

First published by Routledge & Kegan Paul Ltd 1959
Additional material (Part II of this edition)
first published by Paladin Books 1974
Copyright © Michael Tippett 1959, 1974
This collection copyright © Paladin Books 1974
Made and printed in Great Britain by
Cox & Wyman Ltd, London, Reading and Fakenham
Set in Monotype Ehrhardt

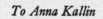
To Anna Kallin

Aber den Einsamen hüll
In deine Goldwolken!
Umgib mit Wintergrün,
Bis die Rose heranreift,
Die feuchten Haare,
O Liebe, deines Dichters!

Contents

Part 1

Introduction

Re-reading these papers for publication has been an interesting experience, I began the introduction to the first edition of this book in 1959. The papers extend over 13 years; from a simple talk for the B.B.C. Home Service in 1945 to a complex talk for the Third Programme in 1958. For this paperback edition I have added some fresh material from the years 1972-4. Dipping into them as an unsorted heap of papers on my table I had an initial sense of bewildering variety. When I had laid them in order and read them with attention, I saw that the bewildering variety arranges itself round a central preoccupation. All the material is concerned in one way or another with the question of what sort of world we live in and how we may behave in it. The 'we' changes from the human race in general into the various divisions that are appropriate. 'We' becomes the West, Europe, England. Or, more often, it becomes practitioners of the imaginative world as opposed to technicians. Creative artists break down into poets, painters, composers, etc. Finally 'we' disappears altogether into 'I'.

The 'I' that emerges is near to what Jung has named the *persona*. It is myself in my public function as a composer. There is little personal anecdote; all, on the surface, is a discussion of general ideas. Yet the book is autobiographical none the less. It is safer to appreciate the ideas as dramatizations of processes in me, relating to my work as a composer, rather than to read the book as an introduction to the numerous authors it mentions.

The relation of the processes, and therefore of this book, to my composition is analogous to that of Shaw's Prefaces to his plays. I can remember the excitement when *Back to Methuselah* was first published. Literary critics found themselves wrestling not only with five plays but with a lengthy essay on Evolution. An ardent Shavian told me that this essay had already become a biology text-book in a Welsh university. It is clear enough now that if this really happened and was not mere hearsay, then the biology students were ill-advised. You will not get very far by reading the Preface to *Back to Methuselah* as a scientific treatise. Shaw makes play with great scientific names like Darwin and Lamarck, but the more relevant names in the Preface are Samuel Butler and Goethe. Butler had tilted against Darwin, as Goethe had tilted against Newton. Both were creative artists accepting the challenge of a divided world; trying to move over from the world of art into that of science, without denying their imaginative sensibilities. Neither of them, nor Shaw, was a scientist as Newton or Darwin was.

The energy which Goethe could spare for his scientific interests is something we can only wonder at. Yet we cannot complain he failed to supply us with enough imaginative work. With Butler on the other hand we can fairly say that his quasi-scientific books are disproportionate to his imaginative work; much as though Shaw had written five Prefaces to every one play. Unfortunately my own acceptance of the challenge of a world divided unnaturally between technics and imagination is limited and desultory. This is not merely because the scientific world has become quite incomprehensible to the layman in its specialization, or even because the dazzling achievements of technics are socially so equivocal that we artists are thrown back into the imaginative world as into a fortress. I feel that had I energy enough I could do more. This lack of energy produces I think a tone of petulance, as though one had a black grudge against the demon technologist for operating his gifts at all. I have not always succeeded in holding this issue in front of us as a social experience in which we are *all* involved, and all equally to be congratulated or pitied. I have gone over to the attack like a teddy-boy David.

Shaw's Prefaces are more obviously related to his plays than this book can be to my music. We can see at once how the prefaces are a true, though subsidiary part of his work as a writer, and we know he could never have allowed them to be printed in the kind of rambling style I can permit myself, just because my creative work is with tones not words. A composer rarely produces polished prose or verse which can stand on its own as literature. He uses words as discourses and reserves the expression of artistic emotion for tones. He writes usually about his life or about music, but I have not done this.

If the material of this book were more directly autobiographical, like Stravinsky's *Chroniques de ma vie*, or more concerned with aesthetics, like his *Poétique musicale*, then all would be simpler. Both the autobiographical and the musical elements are transmuted. This will hinder or help according to temperament.

It is useless to acknowledge all the sources of the ideas thrown out in this book, none of which I would say is strictly my own. My own is only the viewpoint. But I need to make acknowledgment to Jung; not only because of all I have learnt from him but for a specific reason concerned with one chapter. When I was collecting material for the paper on Schönberg I arranged to visit Kokoschka in Zurich, to hear his account of their student days together in Vienna. I was early for our meeting and turned aside on the way, to walk down a little street shaped like a Y. I was vaguely looking for a copy of Jung's collection of essays on Freud, Joyce, Picasso and kindred subjects called *Wirklichkeit der Seele*, and I had seen a bookshop at the bifurcation of the Y. I went into this shop and straight to a shelf of second-hand books in front of me and put my hand immediately on to the Jung volume. This is a good example of what Jung calls a 'meaningful coincidence'. Under the influence of this coincidence and pressed for time, I used the book shamelessly for my own purposes. Even the quotation from Joyce's *Ulysses* which appears in my Chapter 4 was chosen by Jung not by me. At the time of the Third Programme obituary for Schönberg it was not possible to acknowledge these thefts, but now I must do so.

In the Ascona meetings and the published *Eranos Year Books* Jung has initiated a tremendous activity of comprehension, even where his own contribution has been small. I take this to be as it were a movement from the other side. The distinguished specialists who meet yearly at Ascona and contribute the papers are for the most part practitioners of certain scientific disciplines who want to move towards the world of the spirit, without abandoning their scientific intelligence. They are as aware of the challenge of our unnaturally divided world as any creative artist has been. It is a hopeful sign. Recently I found myself sitting for an aeroplane journey beside a most civilized Scot, who was a salesman for atomic power stations. Not only did we find immediate common ground, as though we might have discussed this book together, but his account of how atomic research workers live within their incomprehensible world seemed to me on a par with matters of my own specialized experience. The Scot however still played the go-between. He spoke somehow with his en-caged research men, and he spoke with me. More may not be possible for a while yet.

We live in a society in which the Scot is a salesman in millions, while my publisher's representative deals in hundreds. The atomic salesman, or his firms, can afford to pamper his research workers like the Renaissance Prince pampered his court painter. It is not really a question of commercial economics, but a question of social value. Our society as a *whole* puts value upon scientific technology. It only puts value on imaginative art piece-meal. Again, I as a composer may put value upon imaginative art equal to the value society as a whole may put on scientific technology. But I cannot alter the general situation. Nor is that situation really altered by the fact that science students may be assiduous concert-goers and buyers of discs. I refer to this matter here, though it often appears later in the book, because this distinction between the *social* value and the *personal* value is not easy to bear in mind when, in the course of argument or by abrupt statement, I set out from the acceptance of the social value *as a fact*, to the refusal of the value *as an ideal*.

It would be mispresenting this book to finish the Introduction on a note of polemic. In so far as my job is to give account of the imaginative world within, that is done through music. The book is a related activity, and is wayward and divagatory because autobiographical. If I were a novelist I can imagine the book would be much concerned with an increasing awareness of personal relations. For me such increasing awareness has meant an increasing knowledge of oneself; and this knowledge of oneself has led to a deepening understanding of our manifold, perhaps ever more varied apprehension of reality. I think the book communicates some of the excitement of this deepening awareness. It communicates it not through the immediate image of a piece of music, but through the mediate image of the play of ideas.

1 A Composer's Point of View

'A Composer's Point of View' was broadcast after the news on a Sunday evening in May 1945, in the Home Service of the B.B.C. At that time, before T.V., this was a peak listening hour. Therefore my talk had to seem simple and popular. It took a great effort, I remember, to hammer out this simplicity of language and popularity of image (such as the Marx Brothers and Disney films in vogue then), without emptying the talk of content. What strikes me thirteen years later is that too much was packed in. Yet the talk comes near to describing adequately in general and simple terms my aims and hopes as a composer. These are clear enough for all to read.

Further, for myself, I can find, buried in the simple words, hints of more complex ideas, which only later demanded attention. I find an example in the first paragraph, at the words: 'It is as though another world had spoken . . .' This meant explicitly the world of imagination in contrast to the world of mechanics. But it implies the experience I found later was Schönberg's, among others; to breathe at times 'air from another planet'.

'Ich fühle Luft von anderem Planeten.'

As a musician my sharpest sense is that of sound. I cannot help listening to things. Living as I do in the country, I notice every year when the nightingales have begun to sing again in the wood down the road. They sing, of course, in the daytime but I am more often indoors playing the piano. So it is at night, when other birds are silent, that I hear them with startling clearness, especially when the night is still. The peculiar, liquid tone of their song can sound like someone sobbing from heartbreak, which makes us respond deep down inside. It may only be for a moment, when some quality in the night and the sound of the bird-song combine to make a specially intense image. At such time we respond. It is as though another world had spoken by some trick of correspondence between the outside and the inside. For the 'thing' inside only works if the proper image is offered from the outside.

Of course, it is not only nature and not only music which can provide the image. I am obviously much more susceptible to sound, being a musician. But I can remember on one occasion walking through a gallery, and unexpectedly seeing a statue; and something in the angle of vision from which I first saw it made the moment of impact so sharp that it took my breath away. In this case the trick seems more mysterious, for there was no living nightingale, only the cold stone. Pygmalion carved a statue so perfectly that it came to life to disconcert him; but it is not really mere life-likeness in carved stone which takes the breath away. It is what we usually call beauty, and we can't define it. We simply enjoy it, or reject it, certain only that it has a much longer life than any one of us. It remains like the majesty of great cathedrals, for centuries. Partly it is this touch of eternity which impresses us. Beautifully shaped dishes from thousands of years ago appear as fresh as when they left the hand of the potter, and certain music can sound as though it must always have been there.

Michelangelo spoke as though, for him, the beautiful forms of his statues were already there beforehand in the stone, embedded in the untouched lump of marble; as if he merely uncovered them, by chipping away the stone surrounding the image inside. I think that was really a descriptive picture of his own imagination, which saw the work as finished before it had been begun. It is very much what Mozart wrote in a letter about composition. He said that his best works of music appeared to him all at once, as though the time taken to have sounded them were reduced to a single moment. Then all he did was write it down: his greatest gift, according to him, was the phenomenal memory which enabled him to hold the music he had imagined for days in his head.

From my own experience, as one whose habit is to create things, this process of imagination is outside our control. It lives us, rather than we live it. It is continuous. It may go to sleep for a time – or the pressure of everyday things may keep it out of mind, but not for long. In fact if the everyday life becomes too insistent, the imaginative life inside can behave like a disease. It will offer a growing resistance to the outside engagements. This may begin as lethargy, inertia or melancholy. But it can well end in a real illness. Also – and this has always been known – the imaginative life can play tricks on the artist, by making its own life appear the normal and the everyday.

Perhaps, this invasion of the everyday life by the imaginative life is not so absurd as it sounds. Poetry is made of the same words as we use for quite ordinary communication. It is the sea-change the words suffer inside the poet which gives them the accent of poetry.

> Golden lads and girls all must
> As chimney-sweepers come to dust.

That Shakespearean couplet is so well known and so accepted, that we forget the magic which has made poetry of a phrase so unpromising as chimney-sweepers.

It was easier for everyone to think in this way when magic was still part of the real world; but soon after Shakespeare's day the temper of the West gradually changed. People became increasingly drawn to the world of discovery, of inventions, of technics. Emotional energy, which before had been somehow divided between the real world and the inner world, tended to become centred in the one world of technics. Consequently poetic imagination suffered an increasingly severe deprivation. In order to live it became romantic and eccentric.

Today, the world of machines asks less and less for whole men, more for mass men with mechanical habits. The virtue of this world is precision; the vice, repetition. The true picture of the modern worker is no longer the craftsman potter at the wheel, nor even the surgeon at the operating table, but the young woman at the conveyor-belt, with the loudspeaker playing 'Music While You Work'. The music helps the rate of production.

Just how far this wave of mechanization is to carry us no one can guess. The agricultural countries of eastern Europe are only just now starting to turn the peasant into the agricultural labourer, supplied with tractors from the factory. It probably seems very new and revolutionary and exciting, and releases energies which had got stuck in an old system. But we in England are becoming much more aware of the price. Industrialization is nothing new to us. Something else will be new, but our own preoccupation with social efficiency may well resist it. For if we want a man's work to have again some relation to his imaginative life, we shall have to relax the mechanical precision of the conveyor-belt. But then how are we to fill our homes with all the gadgets we feel we need unless we make them for ourselves in the factories?

The creative artist, who must transmute the everyday for the sake of poetry, is unfitted, by his imaginative gift, for work requiring constant attention to mechanical precision. But so are lunatics, and all neurotics in whom the fantasy world is compulsive. The man at the conveyor-belt, on the other hand, must have his fantasy life in control. The machine demands control and induces depreciation. This, I think, is the explanation of the repulsion and yet fascination which thousands, probably millions, of people feel nowadays for neurotic psychology and the occult. It is a primitive attempt by nature to restore the balance. And the more we seek salvation in yet further technics, the greater this fascination will grow – and the more dangerous. What we need is some experience of release: something which can bring the outer and inner together again. In a primitive way this happens to us when we go to see the Marx Brothers, where the everyday world is once more both real and unreal. Harpo Marx and the seventh dwarf, Dopey, who cannot speak, and act from intuition, are true and exact pictures of our own imaginative life. It has not yet grown up, it can only communicate by signs; but it is by no means merely negative. When Dopey locks up the treasure-house and then leaves the key hanging by the door, his act is clean contrary to our matter-of-fact world of burglary and insurance but it's a true world all the same. In any case it is spiritual treasure. The more we give away, the more is left behind. And if any merely matter-of-fact person got as far as the treasure-house, he would be quite certain there was nothing of value in it, just because it was not locked up.

That is one of our troubles. We find it difficult to locate our spiritual treasure because it does not come to us labelled Treasure. Or because it is not precise and factual like our world of machines. But just because we have starved our imaginative life of energy, we have forced it to be childish and dubious. Yet it is in this underworld that the new pictures are being made. And I for my part believe we shall see the way out more like a picture, a dream, than a blue-print. Then, one day, we shall put our passion behind our picture of a new world, and bring the picture to life. There will still be machines in the picture, but in a different place. At present, I think we are still more in love with the latest radio machine for the power it gives us to twiddle the knobs and get anything and anywhere, rather than for the tremendous possibilities it offers to enrich our everyday lives. And yet I who spend a lot of my time in the world of imagination can speak through the machine of just this other life. And this other life has a point of view. It sees a portion of the truth – but a truth, which has meaning only for persons, not masses. Indeed, all enrichment, all renewal of our spiritual life will come first from persons. What matters at this moment is that I as a person speak truth to others as persons who sit in homes I shall never enter.

Truth is some sort of an absolute. If we begin to tell lies for any cause, however good, we hurt ourselves, whether we know it or not. Beauty is another absolute. When we let the common level of our social life sink away too far from the beautiful and comely, we suffer as sharply as if we took the children's milk to make whipped cream for the wealthy. Part of the poet's, the painter's, or the musician's job is just that of renewing our sense of the comely and the beautiful. If, in the music I write, I can create a world of sound wherein some, at least, of my generation can find refreshment for the inner life, then I am doing my work properly. It is a great responsibility: to try to transfigure the everyday by a touch of the everlasting, born as that always has been, and will be again, from our desire.

2 Contracting-in to Abundance

During the recent world war I was a pacifist, sustained by a conviction which dated back to my student days after the end of the First World War. I suffered a short term of imprisonment for conscience, but for the rest continued my work as Director of Music at Morley College, and as a composer. When in 1945 the B.B.C. had asked me to broadcast, I was very sensitive to any impropriety that might arise in being a pacifist, while talking on a peak radio occasion. The point of view in 'A Composer's Point of View' is not conditioned by being a pacifist in any sense whatever.

Naturally enough there were other people, mostly pacifists themselves, who were interested to know the relevance, if any, of a pacifist conviction to the process of artistic creation at the present time. For this tiny public I wrote an essay: 'Contracting-in to Abundance', which was published as a pamphlet in July 1944, priced one penny. It proved to be generally incomprehensible to this tiny public, for the clear reason that political pamphlets price one penny are usually forms of propaganda and not essays tight-packed with ideas. Indeed the ideas in this pamphlet do not of necessity lead to pacifism. The most that can be said is that they were entertained by a pacifist. The ideas were also not essential to the process of artistic creation at the present time. But they were vital to a particular creative artist, and they supplement the statement of aims and hopes as a composer, which is in 'A Composer's Point of View'.

Years later, when I broadcast a talk to Germany in a series called 'Persönliches Bekenntnis' (printed on p. 117) I had reached the belief that for a creative artist the function of creation is in fact primary through all the apparent manifestations of interest in other social activities; that the artist is doing these other social activities to serve, if unknowingly, some still unmanifest needs of artistic creation.

In 1944 I was less clear on this matter, and no doubt I really imagined that the pamphlet spoke about pacifism, when in fact it speaks about myself at a moment of intellectual ferment. Yet of course (and here the idea that the function of creation is at all times primary to a composer breaks down) my pacifism is real enough, and in special instances of orders to operate the mechanics of modern war, I should have to refuse even to the virtual suppression of the primary function to compose. This, I think, is no different from the experience of artists who fight in wars because they acknowledge an overriding duty to do so.

People come to pacifism for many reasons. My own conviction is based on the incompatibility of the acts of modern war with the concept I hold of what a man is at all. That good men do these acts I am well aware. But I hold their actions to spring from an inability or unwillingness to face the fact that modern wars are debasing all our moral coinage to a greater degree than we are gaining anything politically valuable; so that the necessity to find other means of political struggle is absolute. In so far as that was my conviction during the last war, my refusal to take part was for me inescapable and my punishment logical.

Nuclear warfare has only reinforced this sense of incompatibility between acts of war and our idea of man. It has also forced many fresh minds to wrestle with the problem. Submission of oneself to this moral dilemma no longer seems perverse or ill-timed. The necessity to do so is manifest to all, even if for the majority the moral dilemma is easily swamped by the concern for survival.

This concern for survival may also be affecting artistic creation in a sharper way than any concern for the morality of nuclear war could do. Do young artists feel a more extreme sense of insecurity than my generation did? I do not know. But if it is clear that no creation is possible at all unless the continuity of life in time is postulated then the ideas thrown out in the following essay are still of moment.

Rectification of the Names

A disciple, on one occasion, asks Confucius what he would consider the most important thing if he were entrusted with the government of a State, and he answers: The rectification of the names ... For Confucius, names are not mere abstractions, but they signify something ideally co-ordinated with actuality. To each object, the name comes as the designation of its being. And if an object is correctly named, something essential is contained in the name regarding the nature of this object.*

While if an object is incorrectly named, then we tend to put the value we attach to the name on to the object, which will become thereby incorrectly valued. From this springs every sort of confusion. Nothing is more desirable in our day than this rectification of the names, for in the deepening confusion we must constantly begin again at the beginning. To take an instance: there has been an attempt to prove that living beings are really only machines, and it has been shown that by habitually associating the sound of a bell with the eating of food, the mouths of dogs will water at the sound only. That physiological processes can be thus reduced to apparent mechanism is meant to convince us of the mechanical nature of life, which is thereby to receive the lower value of the machine, and the machine the higher value of life. Yet it would be hopeless to try and train a conditioned reflex by such means in a motor car, or even in a corpse. So that in the end 'life' and 'machine' are different names for different things. The rectification first enables us to speak of them correctly. To speak of them correctly will enable us to act correctly with regard to them – and so on.

Science and Poetry

Now, when value passes to the machine as against life, it also passes to Science as against Poetry. Everyone interested in this fundamental problem should read Willey: *Seventeenth Century Background*,† which deals exhaustively with the artistic consequences of the division of sensibility into areas of 'true' statement (Science), and 'fiction' (Poetry). One of the significant trends of our time is that in films such as the Disney cartoons, the Marx Brothers, The Little Hunch-Backed Horse, the mechanical 'facts' are being increasingly made to submit to the imaginative vision; that is, by arrangement and distortion, they are made into material for another class of experience than empirical observation.

* Wilhelm, *Confucius & Confucianism* (Kegan Paul, 1931; Chatto & Windus, 1934).

† Chatto & Windus, 1945.

That value should be passing again to this other class of experience is a sign of the coming change in the climate of opinion.

The Beautiful and the Good

The value, as a society, which we put on art is not only affected by the division into 'fact' and 'fiction', but is also conditioned by our notions of morality. Thus the Greeks felt the concepts of the beautiful and the good to be so close together that they used the expression as one word. It took centuries of Christian teaching to break them apart and to arrive at a position where, with Puritanism, the beautiful is felt to be bad. But the Greek feeling seems to express something equally fundamental in us. Hence the strength of the humanist revival when it comes. 'Exuberance is Beauty', said Blake. But the protestant viewpoint, by its nature inimical to art, still forced him to equate exuberance with Satan. Art goes its own way and cannot be brought within the Church.

Yet I do not believe that the gains of Christian morality can be merely thrown overboard, though I believe also with Blake that exuberance is beauty, and with the Greeks that beauty is good. In like manner I find the world of imagination to be as 'real' in its own right as the world of empirically observed 'facts'. I can but suffer the tension of these contradictory concepts in the joyful faith that something desirable will spring from the struggle. At a pacifist gathering in October 1943, I tried to express as succinctly as I could what I felt to be the present position, and said:

When I was in prison I was struck most of all by the gaiety and vitality of the group of young comrades there. It was as though having made the fact of their moral integrity clear by the submission to imprisonment they were yet able to turn to the community around them and to live in generous contact with its members. I feel this has a meaning for all of us. Unless there is room in our movement not only for the necessary moral attitude, but also for the exuberance and ever-renewing spring of life, then it has nothing to contribute to the society that is to come after the war. We need to temper the 'prophetic gloom' into which we are apt to descend, with a proper and joyful humanism. If I may express it by an aphorism: the stigmata may appear in the solitude of a cave, but the eating and drinking is with the brethren.

The change of sensibility associated with such great names as Francis Bacon, Isaac Newton, Hobbes, Locke and Voltaire, led to the belief that human culture and progress were best obtained through technics. The result of this was that people came to feel the world of imagination was secondary and inferior. Art was reduced to decoration, and further debased to sentimentality. Either one said what one had to say in exact and virile prose, or one coated the pill with the sugar of poetry. Now, every material value which the technicians saw as springing from their discoveries was realized, and more. What they did not foresee was the paradox that the debasement of the world of imagination produced human beings incapable of using decently the material abundance thus produced. This has reached such dimensions that the material world is now destroying itself. The outlook would be hopeless but for the fact that there is also now a conscious revolt against this condition. More and more people are born for whom the world of imagination is once more vital, if not decisive. Anyone who lives from the values of this inner world walks as a stranger through the world of technics. The consequences to himself may be serious, because instinctively the mass-based society tries to 'liquidate' him, to use the technical term. This again is no cause for despair in a general change of attitude which may take centuries. The endurance of physical defeat by the new values is a spiritual victory, from which fresh spiritual strength is drawn. As an artist I am interested in the re-animation of the world of imagination, because people who come to inhabit this world will naturally want to enjoy its products, which are works of art. Once the values of a spiritual order are re-admitted as valid in their own right for the full life natural to human beings, then, and then only, art ceases to be mere decoration, sentimentality and 'dope' and comes to be the creation and enjoyment of the products of the spiritual imagination.

The 'Torment of Dualism'

The endless dualisms, of spirit-matter, imagination-fact, even down to that of class, have led to a position psychologically where modern man is already born into division, and his capacity for balanced life seriously weakened. Indeed, total war on its present scale is only possible because everyone is able in entire unconsciousness to project his inferior side on to the enemy. A lot of modern art attempts to find expression for the anguish of these divisions, but in the long run this state is fatal to art.

The only concept we can place over against the fact of divided man is the idea of the whole man. (The most enchanting expression of a general state where theological man is balanced against natural man is in Mozart's *Magic Flute*. From *this* point of view such masterpieces as *Fidelio* and *The Ring* appear to decline from the height reached.) If a pacifist, for example, has to contract-out of an intolerable social condition, he needs to sense that he is contracting-in to something more generous, rather as the early Christians contracted-out of the Empire into a new abundance. From this sense sprang the characteristic which most puzzled their contemporaries – their gaiety. Truly speaking, we are only able to contract-out of war into peace. The outward sign of such an inner health will be an abundance of creation, whether of values or works, in a world of destruction. This is why a pacifist-artist can be so positive.

State and Culture

Burkhardt begins his 1870 lectures:* 'Our theme is the State, Religion and Culture in their mutual bearings.' He shows how in the great state emerging at the present time, a moribund Church becomes practically of no account, or is suppressed without unduly shaking society, while culture and the state begin what approximates to a struggle for mastery.

First and foremost, however, what the [modern] nation desires, implicitly or explicitly, is power. The individual's one desire is to participate in a great entity, and this clearly betrays power as the primary and culture as a very secondary goal at best. More specifically, the idea is to make the general will of the nation felt abroad, in defiance of other nations.

Hence, firstly, the hopelessness of any attempt at decentralization, of any voluntary restriction of power in favour of local and civilized life. The central will can never be too strong.

Now power is of its nature evil, whoever wields it. It is not stability, but a lust and *ipso facto* insatiable . . . Inevitably in its pursuit, peoples fall into the hands . . . of the forces which have the furtherance of culture least at heart.

Hence the basic confusion in trying to use total war, the most destructive examplar of power, as a means to defend cultural values. These values lie in *local*, and thereby, potentially, civilized life. Total war, fought for whatever reason, accentuates aggrega-

* Burkhardt, *Reflections on History* (Allen & Unwin, 1943).

24

tion and centralization to extremes, destroying not only local life, but even the family.

In general 'men are no longer willing to leave the most vital matters to society, because they want the impossible, and imagine that it can only be secured under compulsion from the state'. Hence the state is expected to supply 'culture' and entertainment, as it supplies employment, doles, or the police. But while the state can supply the motions of culture in abundance, it cannot produce the values. In fact the bureaucratic mind becomes instinctively hostile to all culture *it* 'does not understand'.

The state may even suppress certain art as anti-social. For the modern state not only retains all social value in technics, and feels art to be mere entertainment, but also assumes the protestant ideas of morality, where creative exuberance is dangerous.

Further, the deification of mass brings in its train the worship of numbers and size. A piece of music is valued according to its drawing power in audiences, a cultural organization is valued for the number of concerts it gives a year, etc., though here and there a bow is made to the real cultural values of the past. Finally the artist himself, petted if he is popular, neglected if he is 'difficult', ceases to be stimulated except by these conditions. Well may we echo Burkhardt's question: 'What classes and strata of society will now become the real representatives of culture, will give us our scholars, artists and poets, our creative personalities? Or is everything to turn into big business, as in America?'

La trahison des Clercs

In our mass society, for a time, the state alone will have means to provide culture on a mass basis. But abundance of state culture, however welcome in one sense, is not of itself abundance of art. In a political madhouse we resort to entertainment as to a drug. It becomes state-privileged and its values paramount. In England and Russia entertainers are in large degree even exempt from conscription (but in England, at any rate, significantly not the creative artist). I remember in prison meeting the general notion that anyone who had a gift such as music, should be exempted. Behind this feeling lies the idea that the whole province of art is outside the disillusionment of the war and politics; is an area of feeling where the good and the beautiful for ever abide together. (Soldiers will speak in the same way of feminine elegance, 'thankful to see a civilized woman'.) And behind the mass demand for entertainment lies somewhere the desire for the true abundance: to drink at the perennial fountain of proportion and exuberance. When the Church compounds with the state and there is a general decline of values with no apparent bottom, then as Gill saw, artists have to contract-out individually if art itself is to have value. In a general debasement of taste, such as we have now, artists must hold at all costs to the best, if art itself is to have taste. In a general failure of tradition, artists must re-forge the links, if art is to have continuity. The treason of the clerks begins at the point where individuals who appreciate these things do not, for one reason or another, operate them. Now it is widespread and not only among artists.

The first issue, therefore, is to replace the values in oneself – in persons: to put the savour back into the salt, here and now, not 'after the war', or 'the revolution', else we deceive ourselves, as so many have, giving assent with our minds but never in our bodies. *Then* to turn with joy to the work of creation and the enjoyment of its products, for the interest in art is now deep-seated and widespread.

Logoi Spermatikoi

The famous Stoic 'Seminal Ideas' are defined by Marcus Aurelius as 'certain germs of future existences, endowed with productive capacities of realization, change, and phenomenal succession'. The rise of Christianity is an example of a 'seminal idea' of tremendous power. Marxism felt itself to be such an idea, though the promised 'withering-away' of the state has not yet happened. Pacifism, also, hopes to be an attitude which corresponds to a general latent desire, born out of the force of contemporary circumstance. Therefore our principal job is to search ever more deeply for the true 'nuclei' of potential change, so that we come nearer to reality, and in doing so widen and deepen our message to correspond. This is likewise a part of the activity of the artist, as in fact this chapter shows. Radical problems have been deliberately raised, not to solve them – which is impossible;

nor to say anything original – for I have nothing to contribute; but because these problems are the very stuff of our world, and we have at times to breathe their atmosphere if we are to see where to direct our individual impact upon the vast mass of circumstance. It is not essentially a matter of book-learning: Confucius, for example, taught in simple concrete parables; Mozart composed with tones of limpid clarity. Nor is it a matter of will in the narrow sense. It is a kind of waiting upon understanding and letting the values we really want live through us. Yet it is also the exact opposite. For 'truth cannot make men great, but men make truth great. It is not truth which regulates the world, but man must take the place of truth; then the world will be regulated.'*

The first movement is a withdrawal to find our bearings.

> We must be still and still moving
> Into another intensity
> For a further union, a deeper communion.

Thus we contract-in to the abundance of the spirit.

The second movement is to return with joy, bringing our sheaves with us. Then we contract-in to the abundance of the material possibilities.

To effect anything at all in the vast decline of value and taste probably means that in practice we (not only pacifists) shall have to work in groups deliberately small enough to be personal. If the ideas of taste we have are true ones, then they will operate as *logoi spermatikoi* and begin to leaven the whole lump. In my experience the ordinary person always responds to real values, if one is not too frightened to offer them, and the circumstances are sufficiently personal, so that the dead weight of mass opinion is relieved; and if one does not confuse oneself with the values, remaining before *them* equally an ordinary person. It may even be possible occasionally to take the big audience by storm. But, in fact, methods will follow naturally once we have rectified the names.

To sum up: if you want confusion and the further debasement of public life, then you will do one thing. If you want order, and the revival of standards, then you will do another thing. It can also be spoken the other way round. If our actions bring confusion and total war, then these are the things we desire.

* Wilhelm, op. cit.

3 Arnold Schönberg

When Schönberg died the B.B.C. Third Programme was in that exhilarating first period when all who worked for it were stimulated by a sense of adventure. The frightened hand of mediocrity had not yet succeeded, as it did later, in deadening this adventurous enthusiasm or curtailing the programme's budget and length. The then heads of the programme wanted to experiment with a living radio obituary, and were ready to give the biographer opportunity and scope. They asked me if I would undertake this assignment, not at all because I was a Schönbergian in the musical sense, but because I was passionately interested in the possibilities of Third Programme broadcasting; in particular in the possibilities, lamentably unfulfilled, that the arbitrary or circumstantial divisions of our national artistic and intellectual life might be overcome in a programme that functioned as a unity, rather than as an aggregation of bits and pieces conditioned by these divisions.

The entrenched Music Department within the Corporation, responsible for the production of all music for all programmes, was in the event perhaps the least able to respond to the opportunities offered by the new Third Programme as a potential unity. The Department rarely rose above the general reproduction of music in concert form. The heads of the programme therefore turned to an outsider. Perhaps this Third Programme dream, which we dreamt then, is in fact a subjective illusion. But I like to think the series of talks and concerts that formed the Schönberg obituary was a valiant effort to realize it.

I proposed that we should treat Schönberg's life as symbolical of all the artistic problems, in the widest possible sense, of the first fifty years of this century. The unusual quality of this approach is that we rarely use a composer's life in this way, where we may more often use a poet's. But it is quite certain that Schönberg himself, composer, writer and painter, was a true figure to be made into such a symbol.

I proposed further that we should treat his life in epic form, as part of the story of the emigration from Europe into America of so many top-ranking creative artists. (When we began to list the names indeed, we were overwhelmed by their extent.) This meant carrying our listeners gradually, over the three months of the obituary, from the Europe of 1900 to California in 1950. Within the series of talks and features which this scheme necessitated, the performances of the music would, we hoped, gain in relevancy. Vital to the scheme was the concept of good broadcasting. Some close associates of Schönberg were excluded for this reason alone.

My own public part in the scheme was to give three talks at strategic intervals. The first opened the whole obituary, and its purpose was to stimulate interest. It was deliberately informal, both in manner and shape, even journalistic. More journalistic than it appears in reproduction, for it has been much cut.

The second, 'Moving Into Aquarius', was an attempt to associate Schönberg with comparable names in other fields and to try to give the feel of intellectual Europe before the Nazis. It had a wide resonance. Judging from the many letters, written to me by the diversest people, it gave to more than I dared hope the sense of being momentarily inside the artist's workshop, and the feeling that despite all the manifest problems of communication and critical discrimination, the art of the first half of the century was real : 'a fact not a conspiracy'. The third was more strictly concerned with Schönberg, and centred round the opera Moses and Aaron. Schönberg finished two acts of the opera, and in this form it has been performed since on the stage, turning out to be a work of compelling power. Repeated performances of Moses and Aaron as they happen, will do more than anything to hasten the very slow process of transforming Schönberg from a figure of dispute into a figure of shared experience.

From Vienna to Los Angeles

The text of Arnold Schönberg's oratorio *Die Jakobsleiter* – Jacob's Ladder – lies before me. It is an important document for the understanding of Schönberg's artistic philosophy – and he wrote it himself. It opens with the words spoken by the archangel Gabriel.

Gabriel : Ob rechts, ob links, vorwärts oder rückwärts, bergauf oder bergab – man hat weiterzugehen, ohne zu fragen, was vor oder hinter einem liegt.

Es soll verborgen sein: ihr dürftet, müsstet es vergessen, um die Aufgabe zu erfüllen.

'Whether to the right, or to the left, forwards or backwards, uphill or down – you must go on, never asking what lies in front or behind. That will be hidden from you: you should, you must forget it. So that the Task can be fulfilled.'

That last sentence is decisive for Schönberg's artistic intentions. He set himself a certain task: to make himself first of all a medium of what he felt to be new ideas in music (his Vienna period, before the First World War). Having uncovered these latent ideas he set himself to systematize them – and show, by actual musical examples, that every traditional form of music could be renewed by them (roughly his Berlin period, before dismissal by the Nazis). Finally he wanted to turn his back on such exemplifications and write freely and freshly with the new techniques thus mastered (his American period, till his death).

I speak of periods, because to discuss his life and times I have divided the span of fifty years or so of his maturity into four. First, Vienna 1900–1914, when he had to fight like Mahler, Kraus, Loos and the others, tooth and nail against the innate if not insensate conservatism of that town. Second, the period of the Great War itself – when Schönberg was fallow and there is opportunity to discuss his need for a school, his most famous pupils and other new composers: that means, Berg, Stravinsky, Bartók, and Hindemith. Third, Berlin after the war, when Schönberg, at Busoni's death, was appointed to the master class for Composition at the State Academy for Music. This was the period of his greatest material and public success; ending with his flight to Paris and his return to the Jewish faith of his fathers in a ceremony before the Chief Rabbi. Fourth, the life in America in the strange world of the continental emigration to California. *My task*, in the Schönbergian sense, is to show a picture, tell a story, give a guide to fifty years of artistic history, as mirrored in this man.

I must return to Gabriel's words – 'Whether to the right or to the left, forwards or backwards, uphill or down.' The four directions to which the artist must give himself, might equally refer to the four permitted aspects of the tone row. Schönberg once described what he meant by a tone row in terms of a hat. One can see a hat from below, above, in front, behind – yet it still remains a hat. The trouble with this metaphor is obvious. A hat is a physical object, to which these spatial terms, above, below, behind, in front, properly belong. A musical tone row is a succession in time – and the spatial terms, especially that of backwards, are in matters of time fundamentally improper. And that brings me to the element of the apparently arbitrary in Schönberg's ideas, which is not really to be argued away by inaccurate metaphors. I think I can give you the *feel* of what it really was in Schönberg (as opposed to its objective value) by another quotation: 'Seine Geburt war unordentlich, darum liebte er leidenschaftlich Ordnung, das Unverbrüchliche, Gebot und Verbot.' In English, roughly: 'His birth was disorderly, therefore he loved, and with passion, order, the inviolable, commandment and prohibition.'

That is not a quotation from Schönberg, but is the opening sentence of Thomas Mann's story of Moses, called *Das Gesetz* (The Law). The story is a joy to read, for its mixture of perception, sympathy and urbane irony. Mann's account for example of Moses's defence before Aaron and Miriam of his dark-skinned concubine, to which Jehovah gave assent by an earthquake, is at the other end of the world to Schönberg's excessive emotionality controlled by extreme formality – by the *law*, of the twelve-tone system. And Schönberg had plenty of serious reasons to give, if you asked, why the law of Jehovah had ten commandments while the law of the new music had twelve tones. We can see that Mann and Schönberg were already opposite psychological types before they came to such tragic disagreement in America, ending up in a *law* suit. The Mann–Schönberg controversy over Mann's novel *Dr Faustus* is more than journalism. It ties up with Schönberg's Jewishness, his Swedenborgian mysticism, his attempt to supersede his oratorio, *Jacob's Ladder* by the opera with the significant title *Moses and Aaron*. For *Jacob's Ladder* was never finished. Schönberg's first wife, Alexander von Zemlinsky's sister, who entered with feminine susceptibility into his Swedenborgian world, told him one day prophetically that as soon as he completed the score of *Jacob's Ladder* he would die. Schönberg at once stopped the composition of the oratorio, which one might say was reborn as the opera *Moses and Aaron*.

This is not the time or place to enter on a discussion of the relation of Schönberg's personal life to his compositions even if I had the knowledge. Schönberg's first wife died, and later the eldest daughter of the marriage died. Schönberg married again, and his widow, the sister of Kolisch (leader of the famous string quartet), lives in Los Angeles. There are children of this marriage, so all these matters must wait. What should be said, I think, is that Schönberg's imaginative life was unusually rich and powerful. Portions of the psyche, not immediately related to musical composition, were constantly being stirred by what Jung would call 'meaningful coincidences'. But Schönberg was of an older generation than Jung. He inhabited the Vienna of Freud. The connection of Schönberg's artistic processes with depth psychology is real, but difficult to make precise. It is an as yet uncharted sea.

Recently one of Schönberg's pupils came to visit me in my home – a man of great charm and most extensive knowledge, whose eyes were still clear, straight-looking and untroubled despite the tortures of the Nazis – a Jew of Alban Berg's generation, a Viennese. We walked up the hill together, talking, talking. Being Viennese (for I almost became Viennese myself during his visit) we talked and talked and talked – so that it might have been the Café Griensteidl in the pre-pre-war Vienna, where Schönberg talked with his great friends Kraus and Loos and Peter Altenberg. Half-way up the hill my visitor stopped. Like every Schönberg pupil he had submitted to the Zauberei, the magical fascination of the master. (That is the most striking thing about any Schönberg pupil.) But now he said unexpectedly and rhetorically: Did I know Schönberg's real weakness? Of course I did not. Then he said simply: 'Ping-pong.' For Schönberg was madly keen on table tennis. So keen indeed that he played for hours on end, stopping for a meal, only to begin playing ping-pong again – and smoking innumerable cigarettes. But he was an acute sufferer from asthma, so that one must think of his voice as rather hoarse and throaty. But hours on end of ping-pong and boxes of cigarettes are no diet for an asthmatic. His health was therefore never as good as it should have been.

When he was first in America he played ping-pong with Gershwin, who like Schönberg himself was not only a passionate table-tennis player, but an amateur painter. Gershwin when he died appears to have left behind him an oil portrait of Schönberg; while Schönberg has left behind some self-portraits, particularly one as seen from the back. But the curious thing about Schönberg's painting activities is that while in *music* he demanded incessant technical studies before composition, in *painting* he would take no lessons at all. He came to painting through his friendship with Kokoschka and later Kandinsky; so that he once found himself publishing music, prose and painting in the *Blaue Reiter*, which was an *avant-garde* magazine of all the arts, published in Munich. The prose piece he published in the magazine is a discussion on the relations of words to music, a problem with which he was then extensively occupied. The poetry that chiefly fascinated him was that of Stefan George. George had spent his youth in Paris and sat at the feet of Mallarmé and Baudelaire. When he returned to Germany he began to use French symbolist methods in his own German poetry – and curious as it may sound, it was in searching for the melodic line to match this poetry that Schönberg found himself driven towards atonality. The decisive moment is the setting of Stefan George's *Das Buch der hängenden Gärten* (The Book of the Hanging Gardens).

Did Schönberg complete his Task? That is, was he able in America to forget the arguments and the techniques and write fresh new music? It is a difficult question. There are young composers in Paris now who say that he failed to go where he might have gone, just because he felt he had to show that the traditional forms *could* be composed with the new technique. They hold that a waltz, for example, in twelve-tone technique, is an equivocation, a confusion, that the real and next step is to find new forms, especially new rhythms, to match properly the new methods. Good luck to them! As they used to say in my country childhood – it will all come out in the wash. One day. There is too much future in it for our present purposes. Schönberg's early music was not written in Messieniste Paris of 1950, but in Vienna (or near it) in the first decade of the century. The two giants Brahms and Wagner were then only lately dead. Their more petty followers were still fighting, but greater figures like Strauss and Mahler were producing music stemming from them both. Mahler was at the Hofoper, hanging on precariously. At one of the scandalous scenes at a Schönberg *première* when a member of the audience, in the expressive phrase, 'blew upon a latch-key',

Mahler came to Schönberg's defence by boxing a young man's ears. I may have mixed up two stories, but the point is that in reactionary Vienna the tiny clique of people who were really to make artistic history had to cling together or go under. Schönberg's first official job came through the recommendation of Strauss. It is well to remember this when we match the splendours of *Rosenkavalier*, produced in 1911, against the emotional intensities, the miseries of Schönberg's early music.

4 Moving into Aquarius

The astrological title is, of course, deliberate – and Schönberg I am sure would have approved; it is designed to draw attention to the idea of seasonal change. In astrological jargon, our present world month which began its 2,000-year life round about the birth of Christ, and is called after the zodiacal sign of the Fish, is coming to its end. A new world month will soon begin when the sun finally enters the house of Aquarius, the Water Carrier. Very many people in the Roman Empire beside the early Christians had a sense of the portentous, the catastrophic, as that great period of revolution set in. Like ourselves now they were aware of being in such a period, and like ourselves they could not of course see very far forward but only backward. Some of the very early Christians do seem even to have expected an actual end of the world in historical fact at that time. To us now, looking back at them, we are less excited by the world that was ending than by what was beginning. 'A culture never falls to pieces, it gives birth.'

My plan is certainly not to defend astrology; nor to suggest that great changes of world feeling only move with the Zodiac. So far as I know anything at all about the movement of the stars I do not think any zodiacal change really corresponds to the tremendous climacteric that came between: that is, to the transformation of Christian medievalism into Reformation, Enlightenment and scientific Materialism. But I do think that our present prolonged catastrophe (moving into Aquarius) has more analogies to the changes before and after the year One (moving into Pisces) than to the birth pangs of the Renaissance. And I hazard a guess that we have more medieval hangover to contend with even now, than our emancipated selves would care to believe possible. Certainly that, I think, is what Victorianism was (something not confined to England – but to all Europe). The fight against

Darwin was the last reverberation of the war on Giordano Bruno. A refusal of something, a pressing something down – a something which no one *seems* to be upset about now. But of course other things were pressed down too. Victorian morals, Victorian piety, Victorian charity; even the last named wanted to press something down. And so movements that allied themselves with what would not be pressed down had the force of an eventual explosion. Wickedness, wickedness! But so it was.

We might pause for a moment at Victorian morals because I am sure they were the root of the matter; and at the real disturber, Freud. Freud was a scientist, an idealist. He went to the battle with the purity of David against Goliath. He looked at a typical Victorian moral picture – the infant at the loving mother's breast – he tore aside the sentimental covering and exposed a truth, which he proved by monotonous iteration of accumulated data, that the pleasure of suckling was really infantile sexuality. We can hardly realize now the violence of the affront to Victorian self-esteem. But Freud was so driven by his demon that he had no time to consider the storm he was creating. He went on to the Victorian father and Victorian money fetish – which he likened to certain sub-conscious desires; and these things have still power to wound. Then the strangest things happened. Faced with all these unpleasant instinctual truths, what was the good Victorian bourgeois to do? Freud told him: he should sublimate. But again, before anyone had the time to point out that sublimation might be only another word for the old morality, his disciples drove him yet further back along the road, forcing him to assume a God-the-father cloak himself and to declare his theories to be dogma. We seem to have come full circle. Perhaps after all no one can really leap out of his time. For, even if he was hounded as a figure of scandal Freud seems to come out in the end on the side of convention and morality, as though Victorian pressing-down could go on after all, in a disguised form. But if people really hoped it could go on after all they were grievously mistaken. The real scandal, the *real* catastrophe of the Great War came and went. What happened to Victorian culture is brilliantly and bitterly described in the preface to *Heartbreak House*.*

Now the consternation that Freud caused was only possible because despite his ineradicable Victorianism (as I see it) he was in revolt and standing for something to come. There were similar figures in every walk of life. Music was certainly not excluded. My account of Freud, schematized nearly to caricature, may already have appeared as oddly similar to what we know of Schönberg. Here certainly was another Victorian figure in revolt. In the very early works of course there was little or no sign of it, but rather of emotionalism, monumentality and prolixity. That was not the real Schönberg. Like Freud he had a further destiny – to revolt, to attack, to destroy, to root out just all those attitudes which he had accepted before. 'A culture never falls to pieces; it gives birth.' It is hard to believe that, when all we can see at first glance is the pulling down, the clearing out of the way. Like the good people of Vienna, we can easily think of Schönberg as a kind of monster. In reality the matter is more objective than we realize. The violence of the artistic revolt against Victorian sentiment was (and is) in exact relation to the amount of hidden sentimentality masquerading behind the façade of fine feeling. The revolt took two forms: the one, Expressionism – which was to try to be truthful, however unpleasant that might be (similar to Freudian unmasking of the subconscious); the other, Cubism – to take sentiment out of the artistic means (that is, in music, out of the notes) and to produce an art of apparent abstraction. No important artistic figure of this century has really escaped this dilemma – that the two ways forward out of Victorianism seem to be equally dispiriting to the general public.

For Schönberg, at least (as for Freud) there was never any doubt. The bitterness of the struggle around his name is witness to his entire lack of compromise. Like Freud he was an idealist driven by a demon. Like Freud his demon drove him down a road of over-simplification, towards a dogma – the law of the twelve-tone system. Like Freud, I think, it was just the consequent sense of estrangement from fellow professionals and the public, that caused him to draw the bonds of his pupil circle so tight. That he exercised a tyrannic fascination over them all is not in doubt. That they induced in him a God-the-father attitude is equally apparent. He paid a heavy price to his demon for his gifts. But it is not the prices they pay, but the work they do which determines the scientists', the artists' permanent value. If we keep our eyes firmly fixed on what these controversial figures were being driven to do and refuse to be side-tracked by prejudice or gossip, I think we can begin to see certain constants. The sequence runs something like this: a revolt against Victorian (or if you prefer, bourgeois) complacency and sham; a passionate search for truth, however distasteful; a dogmatic attitude to the truth uncovered; a need for an inner esoteric brotherhood of initiates.

Now the closed circle round a controversial artist is usually so small that the big public outside easily sees it as an object of ridicule. But so far, in our turbulent period, the big public has never seen itself as ridiculous when it is all inside some ambivalent experience, such as the German public under the Nazis. Like the artist and his circle against a hostile philistia, the bigger congregations draw together positively on the basis of a shared experience and a shared value; negatively, to arm in self-defence against a congregation outside that is perforce ignorant of the experience and which denies the value. The ensuing catastrophes have been so great, beginning with the First World War, that reality makes mock of aesthetic esotericism. For example, because of his distasteful circle which seems now like a parody of the collective mania that ensued, many people find it difficult to realize that the poet George was not bought over by the Nazis.

So universal in our time seems this experience of collectivities, parties, groups, that the really strange figures are those who do the dedicated, difficult work, who face the crisis, alone. Bartók for example. He had as tough a struggle in Budapest, as Schönberg in Vienna. What gave him the strength to stand so alone? And is that strength a value of his music? Personally I believe so. But I shall deliberately turn from Bartók (great figure though he is) because I want to follow my central theme, (the New breaking out of the Old) into other arts than music. I must turn instead to James Joyce. He, like Bartók but unlike Schönberg, never needed the experience of beloved master, adoring circle and of dogma, but discharged all his life energy into the experience of artistic truth. During the years of the Great War he was withdrawn, writing *Ulysses*. *Ulysses* is the artistic truth into which he discharged himself. A truth so factual, so everyday, so commonplace, so accumulative, so boring, that any of us who try to read *Ulysses* with any remaining shred of Victorian taste, find ourselves excessively irritated, baffled, resentful. Not finding what we expected of art, that is, not finding motive and choice and theme and sense, we project our resentment first upon the book, then upon the author. But suppose the virtue of the art is precisely in the absence of these things? Then the matter is even worse. A sense of inferiority is awakened and our resentment deepens. How many times have not all of us had this experience with modern art? For instance with Schönberg? And is there then no mercy? As though to add insult to injury, our accustomed, deepest values suddenly appear horribly travestied. In *Ulysses* they are spoken to us like this – in a brothel.

Boys do it now. God's time is 12.25. Tell mother you'll be there. Rush your order and you play a slick ace. Join on right here. Book through to eternity junction, the non-stop run – just one word more. Are you a good or doggone clod? If the second advent came to Coney Island, are we ready? Florry Christ, Stephen Christ, Bloom Christ, Zoe Christ, it's up to you to sense that cosmic force. Have we cold feet about the cosmos? No, be on the side of the angels. Be a prism. You have that something within the higher self. You can rub shoulders with a Jesus, a Gautama, an Ingersoll. Are you all in this vibration? I say you are. You once knobble that, congregation, and a buck joy ride to heaven becomes a back number. You get me? It's a life brightener, sure; the hottest stuff ever was. It's the whole pie with jam in. It's just the cutest, shappiest line out. It is immense, super-sumptuous. It restores.

Why does Joyce take the trouble to do all that? I think he himself gives the answer. As the speaker of the words I have quoted says: 'Be a prism.' That is: be something that breaks up the sweet sunlight into its scientifically real components. Be an absolutely impersonal eye. So, for the greatest modern painter, it has been an equally merciless pilgrimage. Picasso may begin with a blue period of natural objects. Do not be deceived! The blue is not that of the summer sky; but of night, of moonshine – of cold water. And before long the thin, syphilitic prostitute appears, the white acrobat, the tragically dislocated harlequin. Objects fall apart, to be reconstituted as Cubism. An abstraction in which for the sake of purity everything that could engage our natural sympathy is deliberately refused: that is the point, deliberately refused. Natural objects here are quite neutral and equal. A half nose has as much value as a whole nose. This is what upsets us; but this is the nature of the art. The poet, the painter, the composer seem to exercise themselves only to baffle and rebut the recipient of their message. For their message, such as they have one, lies in just this attitude of truth and abstraction. So in

Joyce's *Finnegan's Wake*, as if to make quite sure we shall understand nothing, the very words are dismantled and re-assembled. The immense book goes round in a huge circle. We end where we began. It would probably be quite as proper to read it backwards. In the Lyric Suite of Alban Berg, one of the fast movements is written in mirror form. Would it do the same for us in this piece if it were played backwards – or upside down? Probably. Take it or leave it. An apparently valueless, heartless art of truth or abstraction, that tells us so ungraciously to take it or leave it, is in continual danger of misunderstanding. Certainly the big public imagines it leaves it.

But does it? Perhaps, in the transparent sense that it prefers the classics – or the romantics. But just as modern art is an art of the naked fact, and of the necessary and voluntary acceptance of fact, so it is itself a fact, not a conspiracy: one of the objective resultants of a total situation in which the public is involved as much as the artist. *Fin de siècle* attitudes were not confined to the handful of names that I have mentioned. The lyrically sensuous Victorian dance music of Vienna, even that went down before something much more primitive from an outcast race in America.

I remember when I was a little boy before the Great War, hearing the new popular music for the first time, to words something like these:

> Everybody's doing it, doing it, doing it,
> See that ragtime couple over there,
> Watch them throw their shoulders in the air,
> Everybody's doing it now.

In actual fact, at that time, everybody was not doing it. It is difficult to realize that the now universal jazz was once itself new and severely frowned upon. It would be interesting to discuss jazz properly, as another seismograph of the crisis. It too is full of schools and initiates and abstractions. But it would take us too far afield. Because jazz is a musical vernacular, it has attracted many serious composers, thinking to find in it a way through to the big public – or just a means to refresh serious music by the primitive. Stravinsky leaps to my mind. His *Ragtime for 11 instruments* was finished at Morges at 11 a.m. on 11 November 1918 (and his *L'Histoire du soldat* not long before). He had begun his pilgrimage from the enchanted garden of the 'Fire Bird', through the primitive puppet world of Petrushka and the orgiastic Rite of Spring, to end on the sublimated summit of neo-classicism and the absolute objectivity of the art work. In the terms I used earlier, he went out of the Victorian garden first by the road of Expressionism, then by the road of Cubism. So, of course, he is a controversial figure too.

One of our anonymous music critics has assessed Stravinsky as a man who was a composer once, while Schönberg he (or she) considers never to have been a composer at all. Clearly this critic has not taken it, but left it. But the fact that a critic is puzzled does not impinge upon the problem of creative artists in relation to a crisis at all.

You may leave it, and you may leave yourself out – not of course out of everything, but out of certain things that will go on whether we like them or not. We cannot turn back the clock to Victorianism through the two world wars. The sun will enter the house of Aquarius. Keenly serious and sensitive people will enter with complete dedication upon the task of helping to birth what is to be; a midwifery, as I have suggested, disconcertingly and ungraciously factual. At the same time we see as little of what is to be as those who passed into Pisces just under 2,000 years ago. Some very unpleasant people faced the future, some very pleasant people faced the past. And vice versa.

The present separation of creative artist from the public is really a reflection of this: that we have no clear idea of Man, with a capital M, to whom we shall confidently speak. A bishop, I remember, once asked me if I could write new anglican responses, clean and strong and simple like Tallis's, but modern. I replied: give me a Christian congregation with a taste for clear, strong, modern music and I will provide it. That, written large, is the nature of the wider problem. Positive art can only be addressed to a public whose ideal conception of Man is generally understood and assented to. There is no such agreed ideal conception now. All is relativity of conception. There was lately Nazi man, with no soul. There is Communist man, whom many suspect of no soul. There is Catholic man with perhaps a medieval soul. Each a value and an offence. Is there a whole man with a non-medieval soul? Or is the soul so ageless that there is no sense in relating her to anything so short as a world-month? Do the purgative qualities of modern art deny us a soul? Or would modern art be warmer if modern man had found his soul?

That I (and my betters) belong body and soul to the artistic midwifery which I have described is our pride. That few of us will ever have the purity of purpose of Schönberg is certain. That modern man can find his soul is true. That art will speak again entire is as sure as the Zodiac.

*In this connection it should be noted, I think, that a positive avant-gardism of before 1914 can become a debilitating evasion of a real response to the situation we are in 60 years later.

5 'Air from Another Planet'

Through the kindness of Mrs Schönberg, Arnold Schönberg's widow, who still lives in the family house in Los Angeles, I was able to read the complete text of Schönberg's own libretto for his unfinished opera, *Moses and Aaron*. All along I had a hunch that it would be interesting – not only because I knew that Schönberg himself gave it a lot of attention, but also because when anyone takes traditional material for his artistic purposes, whatever he does to this material will be critically significant.

Schönberg left no commentary, so far as I know, to his text for *Moses and Aaron*, so it is with a sense of obvious inadequacy that I try to give some critical background to his text, and I shall only do it in the slenderest way, hoping that someone more authoritative may fill it all in later. And I consider my attempt only possible at all, just because the material is traditional. There is something 'given', which is the story as we have it in the Bible. For the words of the Bible have not changed for centuries. They are the words our forefathers read. If they seem different to us, or do different things to us, then it is we who differ in our tastes and manners from our forefathers, not that the Vulgate or the Authorized Version has changed, even if Moffat is relatively new.

Schönberg made his selection from the Biblical material with an eye to showing Moses and Aaron in their relations to each other as joint servants of their God. The Biblical verses which would seem to have been closest to Schönberg's hand are one or two in the scene of the burning bush; that scene where Jehovah first speaks to Moses directly, calling him to his task, and making little of his hesitancies. It may be that Schönberg was drawn to this scene because he felt himself to have been called to the task of speaking a new message in tones which few have wished to hear. But the possibility has little importance. Or rather the problems of religious or even artistic calling and dedication and expression can never be truly contained within any one personal biography. If I thought the sum of *Moses and Aaron* were only the sum of its author's own problems, I would not pursue the matter an inch further. Do not imagine that I have case-book material up my sleeve of Schönberg's psychology – for I have none. I have merely been reading Schönberg's libretto and reading the Bible. And it is the Biblical verses in which Jehovah states the problem that are, I think, significant. For Moses pleads with Jehovah that he has no liking for the task of calling the people to be chosen of God, nor power to move them, because he, Moses, has not the gift of words. In the Bible story Moses says: 'O my Lord, I am not eloquent, neither heretofore nor since thou hast spoken unto thy servant: but I am slow of speech and of a slow tongue.' Jehovah is angered with Moses and replies in these significant verses:

Is not Aaron the Levite thy brother? I know that he can speak well. And also, behold, he cometh forth to meet thee: and when he seeth thee, he will be glad in his heart.

And thou shalt speak unto him, and put words in his mouth: and I will be with thy mouth, and with his mouth, and will teach you what ye shall do.

And he shall be thy spokesman unto the people: and he shall be, even he shall be to thee instead of a mouth, and thou shalt be to him instead of God.

So a kind of hierarchy is proposed: Jehovah speaks direct to Moses, who speaks direct to Aaron, who speaks direct to the people. In the first act of Schönberg's opera this is exactly what happens. Jehovah does speak direct to Moses, who (in the next scene) speaks direct to Aaron. But they *both* try to speak direct to the people; which does not work at all. Very soon Moses withdraws to the back of the stage and gives up, to the significant words: 'Mein Gedanke ist machtlos in Arons Wort. "My thought is powerless in Aaron's word".' And that is really the basis of such drama as the opera displays. To use platonic language: the Idea can only be expressed by the Image. But the Image may begin to exercise the power properly due only to the Idea. If for the purposes of drama we personalize the Idea and the Image, then the theatrical situations will develop themselves out of the play between (in this case) Moses's divine Idea, Aaron's gift of Imagery, and the people's need for both. To complete the scene I was describing, and thereby the first act of the opera. Aaron gives visible ground for Moses's fear that the power of his thought is usurped by Aaron's word, for he says to Moses: 'Silence! I am the Word and the Act'.

And if we recall the beginning of St John's Gospel ('In the beginning was the Word') we realize how clearly Aaron's phrase contains the hint of usurpation. But the people, despite Aaron's miracles – the serpent, the leprous hand, the Nile water becoming blood – still apprehended the hierarchy of power as running clearly God – Moses – Aaron. The Idea still controls the Image. And there the act ends.

In the second act Moses is away on the Mount of Revelation – the Idea has withdrawn to itself. So the Image takes on a life of its own. Consequently there follows (in the opera) the scene of the Golden Calf. There is no thought or argument in this long scene, just display, on quite a Hollywood scale and much more detailed than the story as told in the Bible. When Moses returns from the mountain (in the last scene of Act 2) the opera text returns to its normal argumentative course. The two protagonists discuss at length the epistemological problem. At the end Aaron seems to be having the best of it and Moses is once more in despair. The Image now means more to the people than the Idea.

Such are the first two acts of the opera and I believe the music of these acts was already completed before Schönberg left Europe for America. The text of the third act had already been written too but not all the music. This was never finished even in America. Perhaps Schönberg was dissatisfied with this third act text. It is a bit strange. It is much shorter than the other acts, only one scene. Moses leads Aaron on to the stage chained to two guards. The argument begins all over again; Picture against Thought, Image against Idea. After two pages of typescript text Aaron gives up and Moses begins the longest metaphysical and philosophical lecture I have ever read in any libretto, a lecture which is rather disconcertingly interrupted at last by the two guards who say: 'Shall we kill him?'

But Moses disdains an answer and continues for another half-page during which he asserts that every time the people leave the desert of aspiration, purity and righteousness for the lesser values of competition and various other false pleasures, they will be forced back eventually into the desert again. Then he turns to the guards and orders Aaron to be set free – to live if he is able. The stage direction runs: 'Aaron, free, stands up and falls dead'.

So Moses (the Idea) is alone, for Aaron (the Image) is dead. Moses speaks: 'But in the wilderness the people are unconquerable and will reach their destination: to be at one with God.'

Now, one might say that just because this last act contained an unmediated, undigested discussion of Schönberg's artistic problems, it was bound to differ as it does so markedly from the Bible story. For the traditional, Biblical relation between Moses and Aaron never takes this Schönbergian ending. In the Bible Jehovah gives Moses minute measures and exact materials for the wonderful 'breastplate of judgement', the 'ephod' and all the lovely garments which Aaron, the high priest, is to wear – and it is a long time after the solemn investiture of Aaron and his sons, when Aaron dies on the top of Mount Hor and is mourned by the people for thirty days, 'even all the house of Israel'. By the very substitution of an epistemological discussion for the traditional story Schönberg (in the final act of his opera) clearly takes energy from the Image and gives it to the Idea. The destination is 'to be at one with God' – but God as Idea and Thought. What is rejected as impure is God as Image. 'Thou shalt not make unto thee any graven image, or any likeness of any thing that is in heaven above, or in the earth beneath.' Such is the second commandment. Naturally, if this commandment is kept literally then art ceases. Where an artist gets fascinated by this commandment, then the psychological struggle is terrible. Such I believe to have been Schönberg's. And when I have clarified things to this temporary abruptness, I feel myself a Greek to Schönberg's Jew. Damned by Jehovah though I may be, rejected even by Plato, on more occasions than I propose to tell you, the Image has been for me divine. Not of course, I hasten to add, an Image of God Himself, but often of his breath.

But the second commandment has never been kept literally. If I think of the burning bush, what springs to my mind at once is a *picture* – a self-made still from the film of *The Green Pastures*. Nor is the image only visual. I can at any time recall the crackle made on the film sound-track as the bush burnt. *The Green Pastures* dressed the Bible story in a manner which I must skate over by calling it nineteenth-century conventional; with local colouring. For we see the film through the dream-laden eyes of a piccaninny hearing the voice of an old Negro reading to her at a village Sunday school in the deep South. I believe the artistic quality of the film was sufficient to lift the conventional and local out of time and place. If I am right, it will live.

But of course many things were operating against that nineteenth-century conventional picture. For instance, historians and anthropologists began to care less for what was written on the tables of the law, more for the fact that Moses was able to write at all. With what alphabet? That was the real question. The question as to what kind of clothes Moses could have worn was subsidiary. But it was also asked and answered. So in another climate of taste the Biblical story could look different again: as it did for Thomas Mann in his account of Moses and Aaron: *Das Gesetz*. Like Schönberg, Mann also juggles with the Bible story for his own purposes, which is always with a slant towards the civilized. Pharaoh's daughter seducing Moses's handsome young father (a scene I may say not in the Bible) might be anyone from the Victorian upper classes. And the alphabet? That is there too. Can we wonder that in America when Mann gave his not too pleasant hero in *Dr Faustus* some of the musical characteristics of Schönberg, Schönberg took offence. It would be only too easy – given their so different natures, and despite their friendship. Behind the quarrel lies a dichotomy of taste. Once such vast impersonal problems of taste and attitude are involved, personal intercourse ceases. The camps drew up to battle. I can state it thus dispassionately only because I am not in *that* fight. With regard to *that*, I remain by *The Green Pastures*.

Yet there is still another way of treating the traditional Bible material which I need to mention. It arises from the growing interest in comparative religion and mythology. Here the question is, not what was written on the tablets, nor with what alphabet, but how in fact did Moses apprehend the Numinous on the mountain-top? And the significant Bible verses would be those describing how Moses's face shone after he had been in contact with Jehovah, so that in speaking to the people he had to veil it.

But when Moses went in before the Lord to speak with Him, he took the veil off, until he came out. And he came out, and spake unto the children of Israel that which he was commanded.

And the children of Israel saw the face of Moses, that the skin of Moses's face shone: and Moses put the veil upon his face again, until he went in to speak with Him.

Neither Schönberg's opera nor Mann's novel is concerned with these verses, partly I think because this mythological approach to such material is of a later date. Yet curiously enough not many hours after I had read and pondered over these verses from the Bible, I found myself reading them again, because they come in that strange novel of Balzac's, *Séraphita*, by which Schönberg was so fascinated. The verses appear in the long account of Swedenborg's life and ideas which is given to the reader soon after the novel's remarkable beginning. For the plot of the book, such as it is, is based on the triangular relations between a pure young girl, a middle-aged, much experienced man, and a Swedenborgian being, who appears as Séraphitus, a god-like young man to the girl, and as Séraphita, the perfection of young womanhood to the man. Truly not for nothing did Schönberg set to music George's line:

Ich fühle Luft von anderem Planeten. 'I feel an air from another planet.'

It is the key to his being. One is not surprised that he picked this one novel out of all Balzac. Nor is the book merely a curiosity. The Swedenborgian parts are very eighteenth century – a kind of source-book for Blake. Sometimes the effect is very odd. For instance, Swedenborg's account of how he was called to the spiritual life after a good dinner at a London lodging house in 1745: '. . . un brouillard épais se répandit dans sa chambre. Quand les tènèbres se dissipèrent, une créature qui avait pris la forme humaine se leva du coin de sa chambre, et lui dit d'une voix terrible: 'Ne mange pas tant!' Il fit une diète absolue.'

I doubt if anyone is called like that now. But the story part of the novel has a more romantic flavour and, allowing for the different kind of supernaturalism, has for me a touch of E. T. A. Hoffmann. At the end of the novel the wonderful being, Séraphitus–Séraphita, is assumed into heaven in words and imagery of quite Dantesque grandeur. 'To be at one with God.' The girl and the man, after the grace of divine vision, return to ordinary life with a sense of exile. How deeply Schönberg understood what that feeling was! Not merely because of his political exile in America. For as Kolisch, his brother-in-law, said so wisely, he was no more of an exile in America than he always had been in Europe.

In Los Angeles he lived an outwardly gracious life: a beloved wife, adored children, many good friends. But the exile was in his inward being. 'My thought is powerless in Aaron's word!' Every time his creative gift moved with joy to its work, his obsessive distrust of the image laid a cold finger on his heart. Thomas Mann's dramatic illness in America was not heart trouble, but Schönberg's was. The stroke practically killed him. He was only brought back to life by, I think, a direct injection into the cardiac muscles. When he had regained consciousness he called for music paper and wrote at speed the sketches for the String Trio. He had in fact a few years yet to live, but the end was near. It has already been published in America how in 1951 an old Viennese friend of his wrote to Schönberg pointing out that he was 76 years old. The year was most dangerous for him, because 7 and 6 make 13. This American information seems to have been false, or at best inaccurate. However that may be, on the 13th day of each month Schönberg fell into ever-increasing premonitory fears. On the 13th of July (he had been born on the 13th of September) he kept to his bed and did not wish the nurse, and maybe the doctor too, to leave the place. He had the tennis courts rung up to get the immensely cheering news for him that his son had become champion. He slept and wakened and slept again. He woke the last time shortly before midnight. He asked the date, he asked the time. So few minutes to go. He seemed hopeful. But then he called his wife, looked into her eyes and murmured to her: 'Harmonie! Harmonie!' and died.

6 The Birth of an Opera

I hold for myself that the composition of oratorio and opera is a collective as well as a personal experience. While indeed all artistic creation may be seen in that way, I believe the collective experience, whether conscious or unconscious, is more fundamental to an oratorio or an opera than to a string quartet. If the traditional forms of oratorio and opera can contain the collective experiences of any time then composers generally will use them. I am driven to believe that traditional forms of oratorio like the Biblical Passions do not now always do this, even where individual persons and composers may hold the contrary. I find that there are unresolved but deeply serious collective experiences of our time which will not get themselves successfully into the traditional modes of expression.

I first became aware of this, as it concerned my activity as a composer, when the oratorio A Child of Our Time *began the long process of gestation. In that example the collective experience was partly conscious (the experience of rejection, whether as individual, class or race) and partly unconscious (the experience of involvement in some uncontrollable catastrophe). I was able to use traditional Lutheran and Handelian Passions and oratorios as a technical basis, even down to the use of Negro spirituals in the place of the Lutheran Chorales. But the modern experience keeps bursting out of the older forms. I took a half-line from Eliot's* Murder in the Cathedral *as motto :*

. . . the darkness declares the glory of light.

In this half-line the traditional Biblical words have been changed in order that they may reflect modern sensibilities. A Child of Our Time *constantly plays the same trick. Not only in the words, which I wrote myself, but in the music too. It is even apparent in the spirituals, which do not derive from Eliot or myself.*

Verbally the text reached an affirmation at the end before the final spiritual. The solo tenor sings: 'I would know my shadow and my light, so shall I at last be whole.' This contrast of division and wholeness has appeared already in this book, in the 1944 essay: 'Contracting Into Abundance'. I used there the words: 'The only concept we can place over against the fact of divided man is the idea of the whole man.' And I immediately followed those words with an example taken from the history of opera, saying that the most enchanting expression of a general state where theological man is balanced against natural man is Mozart's Magic Flute. *So it is clear to me that already as the first performances of* A Child of Our Time *were being given, I was toying with the idea of trying to give dramatic expression to the experiences of knowing the shadow and the light, and of wholeness, not by the method of example and contemplation proper to an oratorio, but by the method of action and consequence proper to an opera.*

What I conceived to be the kind of opera which might present division and wholeness is discussed in the following essay, which appeared first through the unusual generosity of the editorship as five articles in the London Observer.

In the Preface to *Three Plays for Puritans*, Bernard Shaw describes the pitiable state to which the profession of theatrical critic had brought him. 'My very bones began to perish, so that I had to get them planed and gouged by accomplished surgeons. I fell from heights and broke my limbs in pieces . . .' So naturally enough Shaw gave up that profession. As he says: 'I had myself carried up into a mountain where there was no theatre; and there, I began to revive. Too weak to work, I wrote books and plays . . .'

After five years' labour on my now finished opera, *The Midsummer Marriage*, during which time I have been sedulously secluded from public entertainments, if my bones have not perished, other vital organs seem to have. I suppose that if I could contrive to have myself carried up into a mountain I should certainly revive. But not to begin another opera! I could imagine myself enjoying rather the novelty of a television set. One man's meat is another's poison. Shaw was broken by criticism and relaxed in creative work. Creative work seems to have half-broken me and I appear to seek relaxation in criticism. Criticism, that is, of my own work. For now that I have finished weaving a magic (I hope!) musical veil to clothe my strange libretto so that the final product has (I hope again!) the appearance of that indissoluble unity of drama and music that is opera, it is more than personally interesting to cast a critical eye over the devious means by which this operatic unity has been obtained. The threads which lead from inchoate beginning to substantial end are many. Of the two major ones I choose first the theatrical.

I felt (taught by Wagner in *Oper und Drama*) that the opera, however much it seems to us a mainly musical experience, is always ultimately dependent on the contemporary theatre. If we consider the main movements in the European theatre, then the various kinds of opera follow naturally. Thus, theatrical classicism meant the operas of Gluck; romanticism meant Weber and Wagner; realism, or *verismo*, meant Puccini; fantasy, or surrealism, Debussy and Berg. (Out of this scheme I deliberately exclude Verdi, because his wonderful sympathy with Renaissance theatre – by which I mean not only Shakespeare but the epigonic Schiller – does not fit.) If I were to extend this list to the English theatre of my own day, then the theatrical movement could only be, as I saw it, verse drama: the theatre of Auden, Eliot and Fry. At the precise time when I began to know that I must write an opera, Auden's plays were already out of fashion, the *première* of *The Family Reunion* had just taken place, Fry was theatrically unborn. So Eliot had the apple (and maybe the consequences will turn out to be as distressing for me as for Paris). But while I was never sure that the verse drama plots, such as they had appeared, were suitable for modern opera, I realized that their verse technique was of itself operatic.

For both opera and verse drama use music; though the music of singers and instruments is necessarily quite different from the music of spoken verse. And in this distinction, I saw clearly, lay the difference between words for drama and words for opera. The one uses an incantation of verse in a magical fusion of sound and sense, where the other uses music proper. To recapture the theatrical moment of Oberon's speech in *A Midsummer Night's Dream*:

> I know a bank where the wild
> thyme blows,

you must repeat the verses. But when the Statue speaks in *Don*

Giovanni, for example, no one remembers what the Statue actually says, but only the sound of the accompanying trombones. So we can state a kind of Rule 1: *that the verse dramatist carries out on the words themselves artistic operations which the composer effects by music.*

I took examples from *A Midsummer Night's Dream* and *Don Giovanni* deliberately, because both these traditional works make play with two worlds of apprehension. And this is the case also with the Eliot theatre, whose stage is generally a stage of 'depth' – by which I mean that we sense, especially at certain designed moments, another world within or behind the world of the stage set. In *A Midsummer Night's Dream*, the supernatural world of the fairies and the natural, if fantastic world of the mortals get entangled in such a way as to give us marvellous entertainment in this genre. The midsummer of the '*Dream*' is, at a far remove, the midsummer of *The Midsummer Marriage* (as it is, speaking always of a tradition, of the Bliss–Priestley *The Olympians*). Part of my entertainment is the interaction of two worlds; though the supernatural world I conjure with is not a fairy world but another.

In *Don Giovanni*, the supernaturalism of the Statue appears only at the very end and we have not been prepared for it. But its impact is nevertheless such that, when all the remaining characters appear for a moment afterwards in the epilogue, Leporello, who alone has witnessed the translation of the Don to hell, *is in a different range of experience from anyone else*. I have used this trick, if I may call it that, in *The Midsummer Marriage*. Some of my characters see the supernatural appearances while some do not; at least, not all of them. Which of them do and which do not is part of the story. The same thing happens in *The Family Reunion* – that is, it happens in modern English verse drama. But it does not happen in *The Second Mrs Tanqueray* nor in *Bohème*.

Now the word marriage in my title can only mean one thing: Comedy. For there is only one comic plot: the unexpected hindrances to an eventual marriage. At one period the hindrances were almost exclusively social: e.g. a well-born girl marrying for love a handsome plebeian in the teeth of a furious father. Very often the handsome young man turned out after all to be very well-born. In any case there was no question but that the soubrette was the young lady's maid. Clearly, when fathers no longer control their daughters' marriages and ladies' maids are mostly extinct, this kind of social mechanism to the comedy is by now quite out of date, even as it was really already dating when its conventions broke Shaw's bones in 1900.

But what is the mechanism to a modern comedy? It is only when I hunt for the answer now, after the finish, that I see I instinctively decided that the mechanism of hindrance to successful marriage, or to any relationship, is our ignorance or illusion about ourselves. That is to say, it is only in the course of my plot that my characters become aware of their real selves. I took a *prim'uomo* and a *prima donna* whose illusions were, so to speak, spiritual; to match against a *second'uomo* and soubrette whose illusions were social. So the eventual marriage of the first pair became a spiritual, even supernatural, symbol, transcending the purely social and biological significance of the eventual marriage of the second pair.

And as soon as I knew my second pair were a mechanic and a pretty secretary, then at least I knew I had a new kind of soubrette.

There is up-to-date drama to be made out of the innumerable conflicts engendered by our ignorance or illusion about ourselves. So *The Midsummer Marriage* may not be singular in that only in the course of the plot do the characters become aware of their real selves. A classic instance, to my mind, is *The Family Reunion*, where Eliot conceives his hero as returning to the family precisely to discover the nature of the guilt he feels at having actually or psychologically (it seems to matter little that we never quite know which) pushed his wife overboard. In Act I he fails; and the Eumenides, when they appear, baffle him. In Act II he partially succeeds: and the Eumenides are tolerable.

Auden's *The Ascent of F6*, Eliot's *The Cocktail Party*, Fry's *A Sleep of Prisoners* (and many other plays) all use this technique. But more to my purpose is Shaw's *Getting Married*, because the hindrances to the eventual marriage of that comedy are caused, if I remember right, by the prospective couple re-examining, on the wedding morning, themselves and their intentions in the light of some book of Shavian moral doctrine. And it was with a blurred image of this situation in my mind's eye that I had my first illumination – that is, I *saw* a stage picture (as opposed to hearing a musical sound) of a wooded hilltop with a temple, where a warm and soft young man was being rebuffed by a cold and hard young woman (to my mind a very common present situation) to such a degree that the collective, magical archetypes take charge – Jung's *anima* and *animus* – the girl, inflated by the latter, rises through the stage flies to heaven, and the man, overwhelmed by the former, descends through the stage floor to hell. But it was clear they would soon return. For I saw the girl later descending in a costume reminiscent of the goddess Athena (who was born without father from Zeus's head) and the man ascending in one reminiscent of the god Dionysus (who, son of earth-born Semele, had a second birth from Zeus's thigh).

Even as I write now some of the excitement of these first pictures comes back. It is the feeling a creative artist has when he knows he has become the instrument of some collective imaginative experience – or, as Wagner put it, that a Myth is coming once more to life. I know that, for me, so soon as this thing starts, I am held willy-nilly and cannot turn back. But I know also that somewhere or other, in books, in pictures, in dreams, in real situations, everything is sooner or later to be found which *belongs* for all the details of the work, which is, as it were, ordained. And everything is accepted or rejected eventually according to whether it *fits* this preordained *thing*, which itself will not be fully known until it is finished.

This method of acceptance or rejection of material presented to or found by the mind is that used, of course, in fashioning any work of art. It is only when we get involved with mythological material that the game is more complicated because the material is so strange. For instance, once I had had a vision of the stage pictures I described above, it was easy to know that the temple was ancient Greek (though the young man and girl were of our time), and it seemed plausible that the Myth being reborn was Greek. But, in fact, I was months, if not years, involved in the Greek Experience before I could follow the thread right out of the labyrinth. So many of the loveliest and likeliest threads went elsewhere. Indeed, I can almost state a kind of Rule 2: *that the more collective an artistic imaginative experience is going to be, the more the discovery of suitable material is involuntary.* The cause one searches so seriously and so long is impatience rather than clear judgement.

The matter is further complicated with an opera because the music is also at the back of one's mind, even if, for the purposes of discussion, I write as though the theatrical things all came first.

For example, when I *saw* that my *prim'uomo* and *prima donna* returned to the level of the stage all armed with immediate experience of heaven and hell, I *heard* them begin to sing, one against the other, in two arias; the soprano's having coloratura, and the tenor's being rhapsodic; and this long before any words were there. That is, I sensed the musical metaphors before I searched for the verbal.

The initial stage pictures always remained the touchstone. For instance, the complementary ascent and descent is a picture of a psychological truth: that what is above is also below, just as Jehovah showed Job not only the sons of God shouting for joy, but also Behemoth and Leviathan. So I had always to consider in which direction my characters went when they left the stage, and whence they returned. And, of course, there had to be more characters than two. I gave the hero and heroine the normal operatic chorus of their fellows, and I gave the heroine her furious father, whose pretty secretary was the soubrette, whose boy-friend was the mechanic. I guessed that when the *moment* came again, the false but magical struggle between the sexes of Act I would be paralleled by a supernatural struggle of Act III between the old father and the whole young world, with the hero and heroine united. Then the temple had to be peopled with a wise priest and priestess, to whom I gave a chorus of neophytes in the shape of a group of dancers who are silent.

By that time it was obvious how near my apparatus had come to resembling *The Magic Flute*. Clearly no one now can match the innocence, tenderness and simplicity with which that mythological experience was presented. If a comparable experience is to be presented today, our different climate of opinion will demand another approach.

I remember a young conductor in Hungary telling me how much more truly heroic Tamino is than Siegfried. That may be so. But really the judgement is a misconception. Siegfried is a tragic hero who, like many Wagner heroes, is unconscious of the collective importance of his actions. Tamino is a hero whose trials all spring from his search for consciousness and wisdom. The tradition of *The Magic Flute* is that of the Quest. The incidents of the Quest are traditionally extraordinary and supernatural, depicting as they do some continuous illumination of the hero. Some of the details seem unalterable, as though the mind always reverts to certain fixed images to personify certain recurring situations. At the very start of *The Magic Flute* this is so.

Tamino rushes on to the stage pursued by a snake. In mortal fear he faints. Three Ladies appear and kill the snake in the nick of time. To use psychological jargon: the patient is pursued by images of negative potency (the snake) to such a degree that he gives up the conscious struggle and lets the unconscious have its way (he faints). The unconscious produces an image of salvation in the shape of the 'eternal feminine', his *anima*, his soul (the Three Ladies). So far all is simple and banal. The matter is more interesting when we ask: Why are the Ladies exactly three?

To answer that fully would need the examination of a lot of analogous materials. I shall cite only one instance; from a story by the composer-author E. T. A. Hoffmann: *Der Goldene Topf*. At the start the hero rushes through the Black Gate of Dresden so fast that he overturns the apple-basket of an old woman (fruitful Mother Nature, Eve and her apples?). Chased off his course by the old woman's shrieks, he wanders along the river bank and then sits down and half goes to sleep under an elder tree; out of which in a little while comes a sound 'like a triad of clear crystal bells'. He looks up and sees 'three little shining green-gold female snakes . . .' It is the same situation and the same three.

I have taken this example from E. T. A. Hoffmann on purpose, because it allows us to sense something of the excitement with which the romantics plunged into this strange world of fantasy. (E. T. A. Hoffmann is full of it.) At the same time we can guess that it overwhelmed them just because they rarely if ever brought it into touch with everyday reality by any kind of critical or analytical judgement; while for us now such a passive, fascinated attitude is impossible. Also I doubt if we really want again to use Wagner's method of staging an actual Myth – the world of fantasy itself. It seems we must wrestle with it differently, even maybe to the extent of being conscious of why the collective mind produces traditional, unalterable images like the Three. So where Rule 2 ran: *that the more collective an artistic imaginative experience is going to be, the more the discovery of suitable material is involuntary*, a possible Rule 3 might run: *that while the collective, mythological material is always traditional, the specific twentieth-century quality is the power to transmute such material into an immediate experience of our day*. For example, Mr Eliot thinks that he has done this most successfully in *The Cocktail Party*. Others feel that just there he has transmuted the mythological material into commonplace, so that there is little of it left to experience.

To a certain extent the opera composer has an easier task than the verse dramatist in this respect, because there is a long tradition associating opera with the marvellous. Algarotti wrote in 1755 (cf. Strunk, *Source Readings in Musical History*, p. 659):

At the first institution of operas, the poets imagined the heathen mythology to be the best source from which they could derive subjects for their dramas ... From that fountain, the bard, according to his inventive pleasure, introduced on the theatre all the deities of paganism ... And thus, by the intervention of superior beings, he gave an air of probability to most surprising and wonderful events. Every circumstance being thus elevated above the sphere of mortal existence, it necessarily followed that the singing of actors in an opera appeared a true imitation of the language made use of by the deities they represented.

If we consider this tradition as legitimate and follow it through *Orfeo, Freischütz, Hänsel und Gretel, Le Coq d'Or*, to *The Rake's Progress* (to name one of the possible lists), then it should be reasonable in an opera (if not imperative according to Busoni) to have a greater percentage of the marvellous to a smaller amount of everyday. That is, of course, in an opera designed to be within the theatre of present-day verse drama, and not to be English *verismo* or English Socialist realism, both successful genres. For the greater percentage of the marvellous will allow the opera composer to present the collective spiritual experience more nakedly and immediately – the music helping to suspend the critical and analytical judgement, without which happening no experience of the numinous can be immediate at all. For example, as soon as we begin to have critical doubts of the propriety, say, of the pseudo-Christian ritual of *Parsifal*, we are provoked, not enriched.

But it is clear that the composer, or his librettist, must be able to condense the necessary material easily and appropriately on to the stage, in something like the way Wagner condensed the divagatory romance of *Tristan* into three acts, where the action is minimal. Wagner thought that dramatic material which needed a lot of scene-changing should be left as romance or novel. Verdi would not have agreed with him. But Verdi might have been more inclined to hold a later form of this opinion after seeing a cinematic masterpiece like *Citizen Kane*, where the cutting and the shots themselves (that is scene-changing *in excelsis*) become part of the artistic experience and put the old-fashioned scene-changing of the operatic stage to shame. *Citizen Kane* is also a Quest story.

Now once I had got as far as this and understood the kind of material presenting itself, and so the kind of opera I had to write, then the nagging question of what kind of music would do all that I wanted became instant.

The kinds and forms of music which appear in established operas have all somewhere sprung from the efforts of the composers to deal with their words and their theatrical situations. Composers collect together a kind of apparatus with which they can do all they want. Think for a moment of Verdi faced with the demands of a Renaissance drama like *Don Carlos*. At one point he has the Emperor Philip alone in his oratory returning again and again to the burden of his loneliness: 'But she can never love me.' (I have paraphrased not quoted.) Verdi writes for Philip an aria in the form of a rondo (the recurring musical theme bearing the verbal burden) which fits, enhances and enriches the situation – indeed, in a sense, *is* the situation.

But, later, Verdi must present Philip, not as the lonely old man, but as the Emperor in dispute with the Grand Inquisitor. (The conflict in Renaissance drama is often more seriously between men's passions and their duties, or even between divergent duties, than between rival desires.) For this, Verdi constructs a musical scheme out of the two deep men's voices and all the lower instruments of the orchestra. Again the musical image *is* the situation. And it is no different when Verdi contrasts this deep dark sound with a high clear woman's voice – the voice of young passionate love. That is to say it is no different if Verdi, the master, creates the music that *is* the situation. Sometimes Verdi, the tyro, fails. But it is a failure in the apparatus, not in the intention.

Wagner, at much the same period of operatic history, rejected this traditional Italian apparatus of set numbers and set situations, and constructed an apparatus which would do other things. For example it would make Wagnerian opera out of the first words of

The Ring, which are a stage direction: 'The bottom of the Rhine.' Wagner has described how continuously he searched for the music to these words, and how it came to him in the form of a low sustained E flat, from the depths of a hallucinatory sleep, long after the text of *The Ring* was completed. The Rhine is almost a personage of *The Ring*, and the Rhine music is still sounding three operas later! This is not Verdi's apparatus, but it is Wagner's.

Of course what has been written above is not exhaustive. I have chosen some examples of what I call operatic apparatus to exemplify the notion of apparatus. But I have chosen deliberately – and there is one other most characteristically operatic scheme which I want to add to the list before we proceed. This is the ensemble; where a situation of clear disagreement has been reached in the story, but where the characters at odds cease arguing and begin to sing altogether and at once; the peculiar flavour of this scheme being the continuing, but temporarily static, notion of *disagreement* expressed in music which *harmonizes*.

Clearly the situation for an ensemble of this kind has to be contrived, and once the singing together begins, the music takes an accustomed course until the ensemble is over, the only really fresh thing being the issue. The ensemble must issue in the next move of the story; and if that move is to be made by one character, say, then the ensemble may leave the voice of that character eventually singing alone, high and dry, so that, without realizing why, we expect his or her decision. But there are other possible issues.

An operatic composer, then, amasses his apparatus to suit his need; either by utilizing a traditional scheme, if that will do, or inventing a new one, if nothing will do. A kind of Rule 4 might run: *that in opera the musical schemes are always dictated by the situations.* Stated in this way, it is so obvious that it seems hardly worth ruling; but it is deceptive. For instance, if one character is winning and one is losing it is rarely that music can express both these characters' emotions at once. There has to be a decision as to whose? and for how long? and why? – questions which need not necessarily trouble the librettist at all. In *Don Giovanni* there is an embarrassing place where Dona Elvira has to be on the stage listening to Leporello's entertaining (but from Elvira's point of view, insufferably tactless) list of the Don's amorous conquests.

As the music is all Leporello's we do not know whether Mozart imagined Elvira as speechless with fury or proudly insensitive. No amount of stage production can ever remove the dramatically equivocal problem caused by the operatic decision in the music.

Applying Rule 4 to the kind of opera I have described as being allied to modern verse drama, are the situations likely to be such that traditional operatic schemes will do, or will there be new ones? Or, to put it personally: did *The Midsummer Marriage* need new schemes? Given all that I have said to date, most of the question answers itself. That is to say, there is nothing in the marriage part of it, the comedy, which is not to be found in the schemes of *opera buffa*: recitative, aria, ensemble, and some Verdi and Puccini techniques. And there is nothing in the midsummer part of it which is not to be found in the schemes of music drama: e.g. orchestral music to a natural phenomenon like a sunrise, considered as part of the drama. The only thing that is new is the same problem that worries the verse dramatists themselves – the techniques of transition.

We want to move smoothly from the everyday to the marvellous, without relying on scenic transformation and during an act. For the verse dramatist the problem is the kind of verse that can sink near to contemporary speech but rise easily to incantation. For the opera composer the problem is to find a musical unity of style which will, e.g., let an *opera buffa* chorus of young people of the present time sing themselves into a mantic chorus akin to that of the ancient Greek theatre. In point of fact (as the verse dramatists find), the real difficulty is in the descent to everyday – partly because it brings one dangerously near musical comedy, and generally because unsentimental simplicity is nowadays almost impossible to rescue from the banal.

The search for lyrical simplicity was therefore for me the hardest thing of all. I did not want to match the strangeness of the story with obscurity in the music. On the contrary: as the moral of *The Midsummer Marriage* is enlightenment, then the music must be lucid. The big moments seemed to take care of themselves. The little moments had to be struggled for. The transition between the world of the marvellous and the world of everyday was now gradual, now sudden. The mechanisms have all appeared before, I think, only the degree of their use is new.

In *The Magic Flute*, Tamino, the Quest hero, is set down as a

Japanese prince, and the Priest of the temple as Egyptian. In *The Midsummer Marriage* the Priest and Priestess of the temple are Greek, and as the 'marvellous' couple had to have relation to present-day life, I gave them royal names, Mark and Jenifer, out of my own homeland. (For Jenifer is the Cornish variant of Guinevere.) But the everyday couple, the mechanic and the pretty secretary, I named more functionally Jack and Bella.

The two couples are tied together in the story by the fact that Jenifer's father employs the secretary and later the mechanic. Therefore I gave the father an up-to-date Americanized name, King Fisher (like Duke Ellington), but which, considered mythologically, belongs to the same Celtic world of romance as Mark and Jenifer. Jack and Bella never take part in the 'big' supernatural manifestations, which centre always in the 'marvellous' couple, Mark and Jenifer. So it is also possible to consider the couples as psychological reflections of each other. In any case the inexplicit social function of my Quest hero and heroine is an operatic liberty, which can be also, in the kind of opera to which *The Midsummer Marriage* belongs, an operatic advantage.

For *The Midsummer Marriage* is what I have called a collective imaginative experience, dealing with the interaction of two worlds, the natural and the supernatural. Therefore there are incidents, details of the story which are ambivalent if not thoroughly irrational. Such incidents (in this tradition) can be frivolous, like Titania falling in love with Bottom translated into an ass; or deadly serious like Oedipus having begotten children from his own mother. What is clear is that such an imaginative experience is not throughout susceptible to conventional or logical analysis. Still less is it assisted by learned commentary. Did the Greek audience need a commentator to mediate between them and the tragedy of King Oedipus? Certainly not. Such rough commentary as I have made to *The Midsummer Marriage* is designed only to show that opera, just because of its music, may be the most suitable medium to hand now to renew the Greek attitude.

We can best summarize the argument by considering the effects of disregarding the four rules I have suggested. (But I shall place them in a different order.) If we forget Rule 1 and allow the librettist to do already with his words things that really belong to the music, then we shall have not an opera but a play set to some music – a subtle distinction but to my mind a real one. If, however, the librettist leaves all the room necessary for the music, as agreed beforehand with the composer, but the latter forgets Rule 4 and fails to produce musical schemes which *are the situations* of the libretto, then the opera is a bungle of another kind. The music may be lovely but is irrelevant. (Rules 1 and 4 are general. Rules 2 and 3 apply only to librettists and composers wrestling with the special dramatic material that I have indicated as being allied to modern English verse drama.)

If the composer-librettist, as we may conveniently call him, forgetting Rule 2, is unable to wait upon the revelation of some ageless mythological tradition, but believes himself capable of inventing all afresh, then the great danger is that the symbolical metaphor will be idiosyncratic only, and will never have the power of a collective image. If, however, the tradition is revealed and accepted but, forgetting Rule 3, the traditional material is in no way worked upon so that it may speak immediately to our own day, then the result will almost certainly seem mere fantasy.

Of course, these supposed four rules are only suggestions, but they enable one to ask critical questions. And though the answers may not be precisely 'yes' or 'no', the colloquy helps the composer-librettist to know what he is doing. Four examples:

1. By how much and in what way is Berg's opera *Wozzeck* more than Büchner's play?
2. Is the Auden libretto for Stravinsky's *The Rake's Progress* really a private world?
3. Is the Hofmannsthal–Strauss opera *Die Frau ohne Schatten* merely a fable?
4. Do the musical schemes to Vaughan Williams's opera *The Pilgrim's Progress* indissolubly express the situations he has taken from Bunyan's Quest story?

All these questions circle around a central proposition that it is really possible to create and to recognize 'that indissoluble unity of drama and music' which we call opera – that this is more than music to a play or than choreography to an established symphony. I have really taken this proposition all the time for granted in discussing a somewhat special possibility for an opera of the present time. For I am quite sure there can be successful modern operas outside the genre I have tried to describe as that to which my own opera belongs. Indeed, I doubt if we ever *choose* to employ dramatic material of this sort. It is rather that it forces itself on us. But once this has been accepted the modern temper, as I have said before, demands that we wrestle with it consciously to the utmost of our ability. Hence, possibly, the contemporary preoccupation with verbal – or by the same token musical and even operatic – precision and with form. For I consider the general classicizing tendency of our day less as evidence of a new classic period, than as a fresh endeavour (fresh, that is to say, after the first romantics) to constrain and clarify inchoate material. We must both submit to the overwhelming experience and clarify it into a magical unity. In the event, sometimes Dionysus wins, sometimes Apollo.

The works of art where these antagonistic functions are successfully mediated – that is, where all the struggle has been discharged into the artistic experience and nothing is left over to our embarrassment – will constitute our ideal. Clearly that ideal will be rarely, if ever, attained. Meanwhile, it is probable that opera, whose contrived situations are fully expressed only when the music is played in the theatre, is a most natural medium for such art. I mean that its ingredients, drama and music, give us all we need to an even greater degree, perhaps, than in the verse play.

Not everyone who read them thought that these Observer *articles had helped their understanding of* The Midsummer Marriage *when it came to be first performed at Covent Garden. Those who were impressed by the piece in performance fell roughly into two groups: those, mostly quite young, who found themselves deeply moved by an experience which, as they often told me, they 'could not understand'; and those more sophisticated people who were quite able to produce a critical apparatus of their own.*

I think the experience which was deeply moving but could not be understood is the experience of that other world spoken of in the articles. 'We sense, especially at certain designed moments, another world within or behind the stage set.' At some of the designed moments in The Midsummer Marriage *the magic really worked. The music and the action and the setting created the requisite image or symbol which constitutes the experience in the form we can apprehend it. It cannot be analysed or paraphrased. At other times the magic did not work in this way. Where the flaw lay, whether in music, action or presentation is not always easy to see. Probably 'it is a failure in the apparatus not in the intention', so that in time we may see where the flaw lies and possibly remedy it. Or we may decide that flawless is not a proper adjective at all in this context. Naturally enough the composer has left this creative experience behind, and chooses to begin a quite different opera.*

One seems to start again often from just this process of examination of a past work; an examination not possible until one has moved right away from the experience of creating it to some place outside. It takes time to have done altogether with a past experience of creation; there is always a certain hangover. What I began to question first of all, when I was truly looking back at The Midsummer Marriage *and not re-living its creation, was the time allowed for gestation. I came to feel that in the excitement of conceiving such a work I had hurried the process of gestation at some early and critical moment. I have described in the essay how I saw as in a vision a young couple parting on a stage in opposite directions, up and down. This first image presented to judgement may have been accepted too easily.*

I have since had a talk with T. S. Eliot on this matter. We both seemed to feel that since opera is an art in which music must finally eat up action and setting (to use Suzanne Langer's striking metaphor), on the creator of the music is put a greater burden of judgement than on the creator of the words or the scenery. Unless the composer has gained some degree of awareness of his real needs, perhaps even of his music, he is in danger of accepting stage actions offered him by the librettist, which would be rejected by a more fully awakened judgement. We discussed, as a possible example, whether Auden had not bemused Stravinsky with a poetic tour de passe-passe, *in their collaboration on* The Rake's Progress.

If the composer and librettist are the same person the danger still remains. One can be too quickly pleased with a stage action which, if adhered to, may make the operatic *solution unnecessarily difficult or even impossible. Eliot and I decided that during the period of gestation the composer is advised to eschew the advice of dramatists and seek the advice of stage producers.*

Talking to Günther Rennert, a top-ranking opera producer, about my germinatory ideas for a new opera, I found myself saying that I wanted to be free from inducing an intense sense of place by such methods as the immovable temple of The Midsummer Marriage. *'Did I not tell you', Rennert said, 'that that would prove a heavy stage liability?' Perhaps if one is moving away from accentuating the stage place, one is moving towards the problems of stage time – or even of time as such. Before talking with Rennert I had been reading a lot of Brecht; fascinated by the techniques of the epic theatre. I find the techniques to be independent of the ideology. I can see that there are new methods of presenting epic material on the stage, which cut under Wagner's thesis in* Oper und Drama *that change of scene belongs to the novel not the stage, and my own statement in the articles that for novel we can write film, but still not write stage. For the purpose of* The Midsummer Marriage *I had accepted and reinforced Wagner's thesis, but it is no guarantee that for the purposes of a new opera I shall not turn it upside down.*

Talking to Peter Brook I met with a direct plea for the use of given or traditional story material, as opposed to inventing everything myself, and for the values that can arise from the Past staged with an intense sense of the real Present. He is certain we can be made aware of the living actors in a special way, as well as of the past story. This plea met with an unexpected resonance within myself.

What this traditional epic material might be did not disclose itself immediately.

7 Drum, Flute and Zither

The following essay is the substance of two talks for the B.B.C. Third Programme in February 1953. The material is akin to that of the preceding essay but turned away from the particular problems of The Midsummer Marriage *towards some general matters of interest in the perennially fascinating experience of music in the theatre. I picked up once off a book barrow in Berne a mid-nineteenth-century brochure, which was a set of lectures given by a von Stein about the theatrical relations of Schiller to Goethe. I have an idea that the lecturer was the son (or grandson?) of Goethe's Frau von Stein, but I have lost the brochure and cannot be certain. In any case the tone of voice was of someone very close to the Weimar circle.*

As I have not read Schiller properly or seen his plays, I found all von Stein had to say about him interesting and new. Von Stein examined Schiller's idea that one of the roles in a drama might be a collective personality, not an individual. Schiller, he said, called his play 'Wallenstein's Lager', instead of just 'Wallenstein', to emphasize that the camp is to be apprehended as playing just such a collective role. I suppose this struck a chord in me, because it echoed my own preoccupations with the intense sense of place, the temple on its wooded hill, of The Midsummer Marriage. *More interesting was a discussion of what Schiller had intended in* William Tell. *How he had intended the scenery of Switzerland to play in some degree a collective role, to mirror the events of the drama. Schiller never went to Switzerland. He fed his imaginative picture of Swiss landscape on Goethe's letters to Weimar during his, Goethe's, Swiss journey. Thus Schiller imagined the lake of the four cantons (Lake of Lucerne) as abruptly whipped up by the mountain wind from a placid stillness to a violent storm, which as rapidly subsides. Schiller wished this storm, seen from the room of a cottage on the stage, or from the auditorium of the theatre, to be the visual prelude to the dramatic action of* William Tell, *which has the same rise and fall.*

Later in the play, when the men take the famous oath by night on the Rütli, Schiller wanted the men to leave the stage after the oath, and for the sunrise to be effected scenically to an empty stage. Von Stein stated that Schiller's stage direction in this instance was never followed because it could not be. It is not viable theatre to have a sunrise acting a role, even if the sunrise seemed to echo in Nature the psychological moment of the human drama.

What struck me forcibly is that this effect not viable in spoken theatre might quite well be viable through music in the opera house. It is clear that Wagner thought so too. The music to the opening of Rhinegold, the fire music at the end of Valkyrie, or the great interlude of Siegfried's Journey to the Rhine are astonishing examples of what music can do that scenic effects on a silent stage cannot do.

But there are other subtler forms of extending, or fulfilling, stage situations by music, which are not of this Wagnerian kind. 'Drum, Flute and Zither' starts off by examining something of the sort implied by some late Yeats's stage directions. Unlike Schiller, Yeats asks for music. What sort of music is he really asking for?

The attempt to probe this question brought a whole series of questions in its train. As so often happens to me, the consequent essay is tight packed with ideas, which are perhaps only held together by the arbitrary fact that they were in my mind in this connection. Yet there is a kind of central theme: the way in which an ancient Greek theatrical experience, which seems to imply this special music that fulfills situations, was quite lost and then in some sense found again.

First I must define my terms – which means beginning with music; but a special sort of music, which carries us into the theatre. And not into any theatre but especially into the theatre of the Renaissance, and of the Greeks and of some moderns. A theatre, at least in the Greek period, which sprang somewhere, sometime from rituals of various kinds, so that a primitive hieratic element stubbornly remains after all the poetic and theatrical work that the authors have heaped upon the traditional material. Hence the title of this chapter, for that already reaches out towards the definition of this special music, in that the instruments, drum, flute and zither are emblematic of rhythm, of melody and of accompaniment, which is what I take it Yeats thought when he referred always in his later plays to the musicians sitting down by, or taking up the drum, flute and zither as a kind of theatrical ritual.

Yeats gave only the slenderest indication of what he expected the musician to do with these instruments. But he wrote words for them to sing; sometimes as themselves, and sometimes as characters of the drama enacted from the back of the stage – voices, songs, of a Queen dancing, of a severed head. When the musicians are asked to sing songs to words Yeats has written for them, then (as we read the play) we assume we know what Yeats meant music to do, even though the melody to the words is absent. When the music is to be instrumental only, more is left to our imagination – except perhaps where the theatrical situation is such that the situation itself makes the music. I mean of course this special music of the theatre. It is most easily discussed from an example. After the murder of Cuchulain in Yeats's last play *The Death of Cuchulain*, there is such a musical moment. Cuchulain has unwittingly fought with his own son and killed him. Maddened by the tragedy he fights with the sea till exhausted towards death by loss of blood. At the end a blind beggar, who has been promised twelve pennies for Cuchulain's head, taps his way on to the stage till his stick reaches the bound hero. And now I quote direct from the printed play:

CUCHULAIN: You have a knife, but have you sharpened it?
BLIND MAN: I keep it sharp because it cuts my food.
   (He lays bag on ground and begins feeling
   Cuchulain's body, his hands mounting upward.)
CUCHULAIN: I think that you know everything, Blind Man. My mother or my nurse said that the blind know everything.
BLIND MAN: No, but they have good sense. How could I have got twelve pennies for your head if I had not good sense?
CUCHULAIN: There floats out there
   The shape that I shall take when I am dead,
   My soul's first shape, a soft feathery shape,
   And is not that a strange shape for the soul
   Of a great fighting-man?
BLIND MAN: Your shoulder is there,
   This is your neck. Ah! Ah! Are you ready, Cuchulain!
CUCHULAIN: I say it is about to sing.

         (The stage darkens.)
BLIND MAN: Ah! Ah!
   (Music of pipe and drum, the curtain falls.)

Now though Yeats has not written out the music for the pipe and drum, we are not disconcerted when we read the play, for we can imagine the overtones and undertones of the situation drawn out to a melody, beaten in a rhythm. We, that is more possibly I as a composer, might be more disconcerted in the theatre when actual music is sounded. For the melody and rhythm of theatrically poetic situations like the death of Cuchulain are imagined by us, I think, as expressing the otherwise inexpressible. It is not merely that Yeats stops his poetry and writes a stage-direction for music, it is also that the music he wants is the ineffable perfume of the 'soft, feathery shape' of Cuchulain the other side of death. And I have deliberately mixed my metaphor between sound and smell for a reason which will appear later.

I suggested above that, at least in the Greek theatre, there is a primitive hieratic element, springing perhaps from rituals of various kinds, which stubbornly remains after all the poetic and theatrical work done by the dramatists upon the traditional material. I am thinking now of the generally accepted views of the ritualistic origins of Greek tragedy and comedy; the mystery of – to quote – 'life enflamed by death'. Music and dance are traditionally inseparable from this mystery, if ever men try to present it, whether it be Euripides or Yeats. From our evolutionary point of view we regard Euripides as nearer in time to the period of ritual, and Yeats as nearer to enlightenment. So that stubborn primitive and ritualistic element in Yeats can seem affectation if we believe only in an evolutionary immanence of the spirit. But for Yeats himself the spirit had qualities, affirmations beyond any evolution within history, though Yeats no more than Euripides denied history for an exclusive fundamentalism.

However, for the moment, all that I have in mind is the extent to which music (in this special sense as I have just described it) and dance are used to present to us the poetic, theatrical moment which is out of time and beyond death.

Yeats was influenced by the Japanese as well as the Greek theatre. In Japan music and dance within the stage play are even now the theatrical apparatus of an unbroken tradition generations old. A recent visitor in Japan described it thus: 'Sometimes an orchestra sits in tiers at the back of the stage or in front of a painted screen. The musicians kneel, sitting on their heels, a row of zither players, half a dozen men with small hour-glass-shaped drums, and an old man with a shrill flute.' The Yeats stage orchestra is more economical, reduced in fact to three players, one for each sort of instrument, but in kind the same. It is much more difficult to be sure that our operatic orchestras in pits before the stage, are only a multiplication of drum, flute and zither. That would be an unhelpful simplification. Western music, at least since the convention of opera, moved quite away from the stubborn primitive, hieratic element, as did all the sister arts. Operas became possible which were almost, if not quite, rational-ist, almost, if never quite, realistic. But the origin of opera in the late Renaissance lay in no desire to exclude the transcendent or religious experience from the stage. It seems to have been chiefly a belief that the coarse and uncivilized elements (as the famous group of Amateurs in Florence round Count Bardi saw them) in the theatre of that time, could be purified and tempered by the moral virtues of the ancient world. This was certainly the conscious aim: to extend the Renaissance victories over the medieval crudity (but of course entirely within Christian tradition) into the realm of the theatre. The consequences of what they were not conscious of came of course later, and cannot be imputed to their wickedness. They were lettered Christians with a civilizing intention, and opera which became the very Whore of Babylon to other Christians later, equally lettered as they, was merely the result of their attempt to revive the technique of the ancient stage. They believed that the highly serious and moral tone of the Greek tragedies was bound up with the use of heightened speech; that is sung speech. So far as I know, they did not investigate the nature of the special music which can present to us the poetic, theatrical moment which is out of time. They did not, for *that* purpose, break down all music into the con-stituent parts of rhythm, melody and accompaniment. They did not, therefore, in any Yeatsian sense, ask for drums, flutes and lutes in their theatres. They used them to underpin some of the theatrical situations – and it was a task the musicians enjoyed. But their more important innovation was the raising of stage verse beyond incantatory speech into recitative and song. And what they made suddenly possible by so doing was to have not only theatrical relations between the various moments of a drama, but also musical. There became apparent, independent of the degree of conscious awareness of the audience, a pattern of keys and modes and measures and vocal registers. Within a century, or less, this musical pattern had so far outstripped in interest the dramatic pattern, that the plays themselves were reduced to sterility. Every reform of the opera, whether Gluck, Wagner or Verdi (perhaps in the end even so ambiguous a figure as Bertolt Brecht) – every reform has been directed, though carried out by the composers not the librettists, towards raising the dramatic interest again to equal the musical interest. Thus the opera could become for a period once more an attempted unity between pattern of music and pattern of drama. But for one reason or another it never stays there. It is not merely that critics and public conspire to reduce opera to vocal and instrumental accomplishment (much as dramatic critics and public might try to reduce the interest of stage plays to the acting) but rather from *force majeure*. The more the primitive, hieratic element gave way, in every sphere where European spiritual life had flowered, before the newer fascinations of scientific rationalism, brilliant discoveries, excellent hygiene and other values, the less the theatre, as mirror of manners, needed the special music for moments of poetic transcendence; and the music of instrumental and harmonic virtuosity was, at any rate for a time, admirably suited to a more materialist age. So without some change in the relations between the values given to the world of technics and the world of the spirit, it is difficult to see how critics and public can do anything but be inexorably drawn to virtuosity of performance, even without any conspiracy at all. It is the virtuosity which is mirror of such virtue as our age of precision instruments possesses. Even where the primitive, hieratic element is stubborn enough to remain, the lack of collective interest means that it is bloodless and debased; primitive in the pejorative sense; while what passes often for spiritual experience within the realistic theatre, is merely the morbid.

But that is to anticipate. The proper next step in my argument is to look more closely at the Greek theatre which the Renaissance desired to emulate. Having already named Euripides along with Yeats, I shall take a Euripides play for example: the *Hippolytus*.

One must imagine the customary Greek open-air theatre, with the doors at the stage back, and the orchestra in front with the ritual altar to Dionysus. But we need to see two further altars in the mind's eye, probably on either side of the stage itself, and perhaps topped each by a statue of the goddess to whom the altar has been dedicated: on one side Artemis, on the other Aphrodite, the goddesses of chastity and of desire. But an ennobling chastity and a frank desire. Although we can easily imagine these statues as stone personifications of enduring but contrary human states, that is not really enough. There is a divine element in each, chastity and desire transcending the limitations of the human or of history. Or rather the sculptures proclaim that humans, within the exalted joys of chastity or desire, can find moments out of time and immortal. Thus when the *Hippolytus* starts we hear, as though the statue had come to life, the Goddess Aphrodite herself speaking in her own person, coming to tell us that the flower of young manhood, Hippolytus, Theseus's son, enjoys such transcendent moments; not however in the worship of herself, Aphrodite, through the consummation of desire, but in the worship of Artemis, through the passion of chastity. Further, so near is Hippolytus to his goddess, the man is guilty of pride. Aphrodite will therefore take revenge, and she describes the methods by which she will do so. So we virtually know the plot when Aphrodite's voice then ceases.

Now, it would be immeasurably interesting to know how the divine voices were staged by the Greeks. Was such a long speech as Aphrodite's prologue delivered in any way differently from the traditional long speech of the messenger? Even if the school of scholarship is correct which holds Euripides for a sceptic, laughing at his gods and goddesses, the question remains for the tradition of divine speeches, before scepticism appeared. But it cannot be answered. It is easier to see how things went in the scene following, when Hippolytus enters with a chorus of youths, going straight by the altar of Aphrodite to lay his garland on the altar of Artemis. For the verse itself changes, in that Hippolytus and the Chorus chant (I can think of no better word) a lyric.

Here the matter is unambiguous. For if the audience is to *feel* the passion of Hippolytus's absorption in his chaste divinity, on which the whole drama depends, then the laying of the garland must convince. And it is at this necessary moment that the verse assumes the music of poetry:

πότνια, πότνια, σεμνοτάτα, the chorus begins. Thus, beyond any curious question as to how the Greeks spoke, chanted or sang their verse, it is clear that in this scene the special dramatic significance of the tragic hero's relation to his experience of transcendence, was expressed by poetry. Even if Euripides as man, was himself sceptical of transcendent experience personified in the Greek traditional Olympian forms, as dramatic instrument he had to present his hero's predicament as real. For myself, I am prepared to argue that Euripides was affirmative towards his hero's belief, because otherwise the poetry itself should ring false. Indeed I do not think a later play, like *The Bacchae*, has any dramatic point at all, unless Euripides had likewise, at least at the moment of writing, an affirmative relation to that terrible religious mystery: 'life enflamed by death'. However to discuss the special problem of Euripides I have no competence, while to propound the critical heresy that the poetry is not independent of the belief is once again to anticipate. I must return to the story.

To Hippolytus, when he learns of his stepmother Phèdre's incestuous desire for him, the knowledge is an unspeakable horror. And so the inevitable tragedy supervenes. But before the mangled but still living Hippolytus is brought back to the stage to die, Artemis, the goddess of the other statue speaks in *her* voice. From her Theseus learns the truth; too late. When the blinded Hippolytus is carried on, Artemis comforts him. He begins his answer with the words: 'O, divine perfumed breath'; probably sensing Artemis as a transcendent paradigm of his own 'soft, feathery shape', the other side of death. But Artemis, as immortal Goddess, may not look on death, and she withdraws. It is the father, Theseus, who holds up the son, as he sees the gates of Hades open.

It is a curious experience to pass abruptly from Euripides to Racine, to set the *Hippolytus* beside *Phèdre*. For it is a great deal more than the change of title – than the shift of dramatic emphasis from the man to the woman; or even than the possibility that a chaste hero cannot ever be to French taste. (Racine gives Hippolytus a lover.) One has to begin at the beginning, for the most striking difference is that in *Phèdre* there are no divine voices. Aphrodite and Artemis do not appear.

This was not at all because Racine had no religious feelings, no belief in transcendence. On the contrary, as he makes clear in his preface to *Esther*, he could not represent Aphrodite and Artemis as real goddesses, because he believed them to be false. He believed, on the other hand, that the Bible was the word of God.

It needs a little theatrical history to get this point straight. *Phèdre* was first given in 1677. But the cabal against it and its author was so distressing and unmerited, that Racine withdrew from the theatre and wrote nothing for twelve years. It was not only dissatisfaction with the theatrical life around the Court which silenced Racine; he was also distressed by the equivocal position of a Christian author writing tragedies on pagan subjects. He still believed probably (like the Renaissance before him) that there was a civilizing and ethical force in the return to ancient classical subjects. But if, as I hold, Euripides could not make dramatic sense of Hippolytus unless he convinced his audience that Hippolytus really experienced a sense of the divine in the image of Artemis, neither could Racine. There is an ambiguity about Racine's hero. For while, true to the Euripidean or Senecan model, he makes his Hippolytus a virgin, he also makes him confess, at the moment of the play's beginning, to a first love. So his refusal of Phèdre's incestuous appeal is not the immediate absolute reaction of the proud worshipper of chastity, but the reaction of someone who, chaste till then, had already desire for another. And the dramatic consequences are even deeper still, because this is really to dismiss Artemis but retain Aphrodite. If, at the very beginning of the play, Racine's Hippolytus has already succumbed to the power of desire, has taken his garland from Artemis to Aphrodite, why should Aphrodite need to contrive a tragedy to reduce this mortal's pride?

This is the central problem, the wound which has remained open, from *Phèdre* to *Billy Budd*. The Greek tragedy has an absolute *raison d'être*. Aphrodite speaks, Artemis speaks. The necessary tragedy unfolds between. But already in Racine the tragedy has no longer this necessary character. Hippolytus and Phèdre come to death through the accident of her incestuous desire impinging against his virtuous love for his Aricie. So Billy Budd endures a miscarriage of justice through the accident of his stammer. What tragic qualities these pieces have lie in a different mental atmosphere. But the problem remains.

Racine was quite conscious of the problem. To remove the divine, transcendent element from the drama, whether because one holds the Greek religious experience to be false, or because one is enlightened and sceptical, is to move oneself towards a world of spiritual impoverishment. As a convinced Christian

Racine could never deny transcendence. So, after *Phèdre* there are no more pagan tragedies, only Biblical ones. It is only after a twelve-year silence that we get *Esther*, written for a fashionable girls' convent.

Now the cardinal place in the preface to *Esther* is that where Racine explains that he felt he was at last truly imitating the Greek theatre for two reasons. First that the scenes of his subject, taken as they were from the Bible, the word of God, had been, so to speak, prepared for him by God Himself. 'Je pourrais remplir toute mon action avec les seules scènes que Dieu lui-même, pour ainsi dire, a preparées.' Second, that having thus established the transcendent element, necessarily, for Christian reasons, excluded from *Phèdre*, he was able to use a Chorus (excluded equally from *Phèdre*), because at last he needed it, to express just this transcendence. That he could '. . . comme dans les anciennes tragèdies grecques . . . employer à chanter les louanges du vrai Dieu cette partie du choeur que les païens employaient à chanter les louanges de leurs fausses divinités.'

And the truly fascinating matter is that for his chorus Racine used lyric poetry, which had to be sung. So, once the conditions were given in which the transcendent element needed to be affirmed upon the stage and within the drama, the old amalgam of poetry and music returned to power.

It has been left to our later evolutionary, technological age, whether in its optimistic or pessimistic habit, to have as much difficulty in accepting Racine's Christian poetic transcendence, as Euripides' pagan. We therefore have had to base our critical values on a kind of amputation. We have needed to abstract the poetry of, say, the *Divina Commedia* from the belief; to abstract the dramatic technique from the contents of the story. We (or most of us) cannot choose between *Phèdre* and *Esther* for reasons of faith. Or rather, to put it more carefully, if we choose between the plays, we do so for different reasons. Since we live in a world where social value is given to experiences of technics rather than of the spirit, we, whether individually convinced Christians or pagans, are not making a comparable choice to that which Racine made, when he silenced himself for twelve years. All I am suggesting here is that because *Esther* demanded from Racine the dramatic experience of transcendence, where *Phèdre* did not, the poetry is different. In *Esther* there are lyric choruses, which have to be sung. But when Hippolytus gives up the ghost in *Phèdre* he does not begin with the words: 'O, divine perfumed breath', for he sees no 'soft, feathery shape' of himself the other side of death. Nor therefore did Racine need to tell the musicians to take up the drum, flute and zither and play music of pipe and drum.

If we skip from Racine a hundred years to Goethe then the scene is both changed and not changed. From the special point of view of this paper the most obvious change is that in those hundred years music had developed into a noble and independent art; to such a degree that the word music comes to mean no longer a traditional association with the poetic element in the theatre, whether in the ritual Greek theatre or in the Christian Mass, but an art of pure sound in its own right. At that period, when Beethoven's symphonies were being created, it might be said that the conscious dramatic problem was not at all the possibility of a musical pattern within a verse drama, such as Mr Eliot for all our sakes discusses it now, but the possibility of a dramatic pattern within a musical piece. I realize I am putting this point rather crudely; but I think that just this exaggeration can help us to feel what was new in the European art of music. For it is new; there was no art of pure music in that sense before, and I am certain that no archaeological discovery will show there ever has been. Why, and even how in any precise sense, this grace of the discovery of a new art should have descended on the European spirit over the long period from the medieval *organum* to the so-called classical symphony, is a mystery. But once it had happened and had flowered when it did flower, then the accidents of the historic period, or other rhythms of the European spirit, impinged at once upon music, as upon every one of the other arts. That is to say, that when music as an independent art flowered at the end of the eighteenth century, the European climate of opinion was already deeply involved in the swift and shattering process by which value was going over from the world of imagination to the world of technics. And the artistic consequences of the depreciation of value given to the imaginative world, meant that the effort of imaginative creation began to assume, already in Beethoven's time, that superhuman quality, that desperate struggle to restore the spiritual order by increasingly transcendent and extraordinary works of art. At first the discovery of the fascinating and fantastic dream world of the Romantic movement seemed to suggest that salvation lay in a flight from technics into fantasy. The new art of music, just because of the unrealistic nature of its medium, appeared as though designed by history to be the paragon of romantic virtue. It was the romantic art *per se*. But when the first phase of the Romantic movement passed and the spiritual disillusion returned and deepened, and later, when it seemed possible that a way forward lay in attempting to take the citadel of technics by artistic storm, then music has probably been the least successful art for this purpose, and architecture (I am thinking of the Bauhaus, and Le Corbusier) may have become the most.

Is it not possible that Goethe disliked Beethoven's music not merely for reasons of his older age and of his temperament, but because he sensed deeper down, that the symphonic drama, the dramatically conceived musical symphony, had no need of verse or poetry, and the prose or verse drama had no traditional place for independent music of Beethoven's kind? This has been the perennial problem for opera, and it was certainly not for such tremendous personalities as Goethe and Beethoven to become a sort of super Gilbert and Sullivan. The time was as unripe for such a union as the temperamental situation was intractable. Beethoven did not set Goethe's *Iphigenie* to music, because fundamentally there was no need of it.

Now the *Iphigenie* is the point where it *appears* as if some of the scene had not seriously changed in the hundred years since Racine. Like Racine's *Phèdre*, Goethe's *Iphigenie auf Tauris* is an adaptation from Euripides. Like Racine, Goethe dispenses with the Greek gods (in this case Athene) and like Racine thereby reduces the mythological element to the inexplicable. But not for Racine's reason. Racine, in his Christian faith, knew the Greek gods to be false. Goethe had not Racine's Christian assurance, though he certainly had assurance of transcendence in some form, but he so radically altered the dramatic quality of the Euripides' story that any *deus ex machina* was otiose. Goethe makes his *Iphigenie* so naturally humane that it is impossible to think of her as ever sacrificing any human whatever because commanded by a goddess, let alone her own brother, Orestes. Not because, like the Euripidean heroine, she is capable of risking everything in a Greek trick, daring Athene to give the lie to Apollo (they were brother and sister too), but because, as conceived by Goethe, she equates the divine with the absence of all traditional sacrifice whatever. So we experience, in the Goethe play, less a passionate and dramatic conflict of morals or customs, than a lyrical atmosphere of unshakeable goodness. This lyrical quality is practically all-pervasive, rocked to the music of the crystalline verse. There is no tragic element; no 'life enflamed by death'; no 'soft, feathery shape' beyond death; no music of pipe and drum at the moment of passing; and, *a fortiori*, no room for the music of Beethoven.

What radically changes the scene in the hundred years after Goethe is a double process. Racine, as we know, turned away from the Greek myths to the Bible, to what was for him the word of God; thereby believing he solved the problem of true transcendence within the theatre. The double process which seems to eat away Racine's solution, nearly reverse his judgement, is on one side that analytical temper of the mind by which the Christian tradition itself fell to pieces, towards a non-transcendental world of absolute immanence, or into a world of technics; and on the other, that anthropological, archaeological temper which made a historically imaginative sense of Greek religious transcendence once more possible.

Some of the process by which the Bible changed from the word of God, in Racine's sense, into a book of inspired literature had indeed taken place by the time Goethe wrote his *Iphigenie*. But it was very much hastened in the century that followed. We do not *expect* to find Christian transcendence, or even any transcendence at all, expressed directly in the theatre of Chekov, Ibsen or Shaw. We expect rather the expression of human relations within the appropriate social problems; or even the discussion of social problems through the relationships. Christian transcendence appears explicitly in Shaw's *St Joan*. That is to say, Joan is shown as a person who has experienced it immediately. But her personal life, her sainthood, the problems of Church and State are all dramatized, however skilfully and passionately, with a humane tolerance worthy of a historian like Burkhardt, or of a novelist like George Eliot. Shaw accepts Joan's sainthood as a fact, but he is not himself involved with Joan's God in any comparable sense to how Racine was. The nearest Shaw comes to needing music (the special music out of time and place) to express Joan's divine voices, is the scene in Rheims Cathedral with the bells. But it is sentimental not numinous. In the sense I have given to the word music for the purposes of this essay, there is no music at all in this theatre.

Now playwrights, like Shaw, because it was the temper of their time, could accept the Bible as inspired literature. Anthropologists, like Frazer, meanwhile, began to look at it rather as a compendium of customs and rituals, and produced the necessary apparatus of comparative research to make their point. The two attitudes inhabited the same climate of opinion. One feels a wide-reading humanist like Shaw read *The Golden Bough*, if not so certainly Frazer's *Folk-lore in the Old Testament*. But he does not seem to have been interested, in the sense that it affected his writings, by the anthropological and archaeological research on Greek material. The time was not ripe. The Greek scholars, like Jane Harrison, who uncovered, with a growing sense of excitement, the older, dynamic rituals behind the later Olympian façade, worked, for the most part, on the side-lines of public interests. Was this because the evolutionary, immanentist world of *Back to Methuselah*, or the materialist philosophy behind *Man and the Masses*, had no sense of, was unprepared for, even unconsciously frightened of any transcendence that might be active? For Jane Harrison was certainly reaching through to the transcendent images of Greek mythology. And a more tremendous figure had appeared earlier – Friedrich Nietszche.

Nietszche was perhaps the first great European to be aware that he had, in his own person, experienced the rebirth of an ancient god – of Zarathustra. The impact of the experience was so violent that he became eventually clinically insane. But it can be shown, I think, that hidden in Zarathustra is an earlier meeting of Nietszche with yet another god – with Dionysus, the god who came from the East into Greece to force his way like a wild storm into the measured climate of the Olympian system. (It is all described in the *Bacchae* of Euripides.) If Nietszche in the end succumbed to the storm of the god, Jane Harrison managed to keep her head within the great wind. But she experienced enough to believe that only by examination of the dionysiac attack on the Olympians, and of the allied cult of Orpheus, and more still, of the older rituals that lay before Homer, could any real sense be made of the how and the why of the transcendent images in Greek life and the Greek theatre. Her books have the passionate excitement of someone under an influence, of someone, despite all the scholarship, possessed. I doubt if many can read *Themis* without being affected by this sense of possession. By the time of the second edition in 1911, as she says herself, the battle had been won. The primitive ritual element in the Greek drama had been accepted for what it was, and the reality of a Greek sense of transcendence understood. If, by 1911, these things were accepted by scholars, by 1953 their range of effectiveness is vastly wider. Where Racine in his time held the Greek gods to be false, they would appear *now* to have been true, within their own sphere and period of efficacy. That is to say, if a strict Christian judges nowadays the Greek religious experience in the terms of Racine, he is the real stranger in the present world of opinion; but in Racine's century it would have been the reverse.

Now, though I began this discussion with Yeats and my title is taken from Yeats, and in Yeats's last plays the primitive, ritualistic element is clear for all to see – positively affirmed; yet Mr T. S. Eliot is the real figure for the completion of my argument. Eliot is someone we imagine as wholly within the Christian experience, but in *The Family Reunion* he uses a Greek myth, as Racine and Goethe do, though not like them on a stage set in a scene of ancient Greece; for *The Family Reunion* is set in a scene of the present day. As if to emphasize a further difference from Racine and Goethe, Eliot does not dismiss as they did, if for different reasons, the Greek religious experience from his stage, but by a wonderful *tour de force* introduces the Eumenides into an English drawing-room. Furthermore, Mr Eliot is more acutely aware than anyone else in this country, perhaps indeed in all Europe, of all the considerations I have been trying to set out: the general spiritual impoverishment of our life; the problem of a dismembered Christianity; the problem of the transcendent experience *per se*; the problem of poetry and belief; the special problem of the music of poetry in the theatre. I have little to contribute except the more special problem still of the music of instruments and voices in the theatre. And the possibly strange fact that I have affirmations, though not theologically Christian, which set me in some other place than optimistically or pessi- mistically bounded by our immanentist world of technics. So I am fairly sure that where my appreciations differ from Mr Eliot, any difference which is vital will spring from these affirmations. That is, I may have an affirmative reaction to experiences, which he might have to reject, like Racine before him, as theologically false. All the rest will be my lack of sensibility.

True to his acute awareness of what is involved, Mr Eliot has reconsidered *The Family Reunion* in a lecture at Harvard in 1950, reprinted in this country as *Poetry and Drama*. The words where Mr Eliot first alludes to the two appearances of the Eumenides come within a general discussion of versification, and this is how they run:

> Furthermore, I had in two passages used the device of a lyrical duet further isolated from the rest of the dialogue by being written in shorter lines with only two stresses. These passages . . . are so remote from the necessity of the action that they are hardly more than passages of poetry which might be spoken by anybody; they are too much like operatic arias. The member of the audience, if he enjoys this sort of thing, is putting up with a suspension of the action in order to enjoy a poetic fantasia.

The more I re-read this passage, the more it fascinates me. For I am certainly a member of the audience that enjoys this sort of thing. Is it just because I enjoy opera and operatic arias? In a sense that is part of the reason. In opera the aria and the ensemble are generally placed where the action is halted to savour a situation; though of course there are arias and ensembles which progress from one state to another in the manner of the Choruses of the *Bacchae*. To members of his audience who like opera, Mr Eliot's rejection of his lyrically suspended moments in favour of continuous attention to the needs of the action may reduce enjoyment, not increase it. Or to put it more generally, I can believe that when the verse drama moves thus towards opera our whole theatre gains; especially if our contemporary opera could catch up on itself and come closer in some other ways to the verse drama. I can believe that by just such operatic tricks as lyrical suspension of the action to savour a situation, the play can be given new dimensions perhaps more naturally than by vigorous effort to make the verse play act like a prosaic one.

But if – and this is the core of the matter – if the lyrical suspension of action corresponds to a moment out of time, ineffable, when we have been made ready to see, however through a glass darkly, an image of transcendence, then suspension of action is essential. And to enhance or extend the moment there is little to do beyond calling for the music of flute and drum, just as Yeats does at the timeless moment when Cuchulain's soul leaves the hero's strong body for 'the soft, feathery shape' of itself beyond death.

Now I know that the two appearances of the Eumenides in *The Family Reunion* were for me such timeless moments. I was in no way *conscious* of suspended action to hear an aria sung, to 'enjoy a poetic fantasia', for when They came, I trembled.

> That apprehension deeper than all sense,
> Deeper than the sense of smell, but like a smell
> In that it is undescribable, a sweet and bitter smell,
> From another world. I know it, I know it!

As Harry spoke these words, I suppose I imagined I spoke them with him. For they were in no way new, in no way strange, but expected, though unexpected. I can imagine that members of an ancient Greek audience, who enjoyed this sort of thing, found Hippolytus's words equally expected and unexpected, when he smelt the ineffable perfume of his goddess. Nor do I think it is only because I am physiologically short-sighted that I was careless of what in *The Family Reunion* the Eumenides looked like in the window embrasure; though that seems to have worried everyone else, if Mr Eliot's own concern is general not idiosyncratic.

Having now read the printed play, I have been able to consider the musical, poetical means by which I was prepared to receive this deeper apprehension when it came. But all examination of the technique pales before the fact – that such a deeper apprehension is possible at all, in this immanentist world. Also I could, I think, undertake to show that Harry, in his mental and spiritual distress, is a true hero of our day – prig or not. I mean that Mr Eliot's later judgement that Harry is an insufferable prig is, to many of us, as beside the point as to judge the Greek Hippolytus to be a prude in secret search of seduction. Furthermore, I must confess that the sense of affirmation which was most certainly gratified by the deeper apprehension of these two timeless moments in modern verse drama, has not been diminished for me by any distress that I cannot analyse them down into intellectual counters; nor that I did not relate them in any way, then or since, to questions of theological truth and falsehood.

The miracle was the fact. The renewable excitement is the

sense that suddenly for a time the poetry and the belief can be again one. And so my judgement is heretical in every sense, heretical perhaps from a Christian point of view, heretical in that I did not aesthetically separate the poetry from the transcendent emotion which it produced. It must wait now to see whether after all we are forced to relax our analytical preoccupations, and to accept our artistic miracles under the guise in which they come. I am prepared to wager that despite all the undramatic nature of Yeats's late plays, and despite all the animadversions of that kind which Mr Eliot makes against *The Family Reunion*, these works will stand when others fall; by virtue of those lyrical suspensions of action, when we apprehend the ineffable perfume from another world and the musicians must take up the traditional pipe and drum.

8 What Do We Perceive in Modern Art

Anton Ehrenzweig is a disciple of Freud and an amateur of Schönberg, while I am rather a disciple of Jung and a lover of Stravinsky. Therefore, at first glance, I am *not* a fair person to be discussing the ideas in his book *The Psycho-Analysis of Artistic Vision and Hearing.** I am doing so solely because I have in fact read it all with attention and profit: indeed with much more than profit, with that extra excitement that comes only when we read something which is clearly and truly perceptive – which opens in the mind a window on to a new mental landscape.

It may be that we are stupid to ask for graces of style from books on psychology. Generally we put up with these barbarous jargons for the sake of their experienced therapeutic value – a value which we then tend to let flow over the jargon, like the warmth of a personality overcoming a facial disfigurement. Also beyond the tremendous urge of therapeutic needs, some of us learn these jargons for the sake of communication. A creative artist may come to live on some common ground between opposite truths. If Mrs Maclean and Mrs Petrov both were drawn to follow their traitor husbands, because they are wives to husbands, then we catch sight of just that middle ground where grow such rank weeds and fair flowers of our human nature, deeper rooted than the present convictions of ideological warfare and which a dramatist might not be willing to despise. But I am not by this suggesting that convictions, old and new, are not weeds rank enough to be infinitely tenacious, flowers fair enough to fight brutally for. It is simply that by putting it just in this way, I have shifted value from conviction (or from therapy or from science) over to perception and communication. Because while Anton Ehrenzweig remains a scientist and a therapist, and I remain a creative artist, it is only by lifting over Ehrenzweig's scientific perceptions on to *my*

* London, Routledge & Kegan Paul, 1954.

ground, that I am able to discuss them now. I want to describe the kind of window which reading his book can open in the mind, and to give hints of the kind of landscape (no – seascape might be a better metaphor!) which one would be looking out upon.

For I am glad to say that it is upon a great wide sea that this book looks, for all its technical title. And Ehrenzweig takes a long view. His is the sort of book which Yeats (had he lived at a little later date) might have read and profited from, instead of the books he did read which were maybe much less scientific; but out of which he certainly got part of the stimulus to such poetry as:

> Turning and turning in the widening gyre
> The falcon cannot hear the falconer.
> Things fall apart; the centre cannot hold;
> Mere anarchy is loosed upon the world,
> The blood-dimmed tide is loosed, and everywhere
> The ceremony of innocence is drowned;
> The best lack all conviction, while the worst
> Are full of passionate intensity.

And having prepared us by that first tremendous strophe of *The Second Coming*, Yeats continues:

> Surely some revelation is at hand;

which emotional notion is not entirely absent from Ehrenzweig's book, I am glad to say. However precisely we build the walls of our particular interests and techniques, the tidal waves of the general attitudes wash over them and seep under them. Ehrenzweig himself discusses for a moment the origin of the once universally general attitude of belief that Nature, with a capital N, conforms to absolute laws, discovered for us by Science, with a capital S. He suggests that the breakdown of the medieval general attitude of belief in and preoccupation with the law of God, led at once to the need to transfer the notion of law over from the moral law, as of the Ten Commandments, into natural law.

But now, when the Laws of Newton are tending to melt away into a general theory of relativity (when the laws vary according to where you happen to be when you observe them); or when these laws are being degraded from their old absolute nature to the lesser status of statistical probabilities, then these old laws of

Nature can no longer hold the moral value. No wonder then that there is general dislocation of centre.

> Turning and turning in the widening gyre
> The falcon cannot hear the falconer.

for

> Things fall apart, the centre cannot hold;
> Mere anarchy is loosed upon the world.

And if one is not an Einstein stretching a unique mind to its uttermost to bring the anarchy anew into order; or if one is not able to wall oneself up in an older fundamentalism, from the Bible or the Koran; or if one does not receive divine messages from the Collective Unconscious; then indeed one has cause to be dislocated, and what then can a mere mortal do? I am afraid he, or we, can gang up into groups and congregations and elect a leader, on whom to project the notion of a centre, and who will speak as falconer to falcon, as teacher to disciple, as God to creature. And I mean not only a social or political leader. It happens everywhere, great or small; for instance in the world of sport; and, I am afraid, even in the world of psychoanalytical therapy, and certainly in the world of music.

Now the composer-hero of Ehrenzweig's book is Schönberg; a man who, I think, experienced this dislocation of centre most courageously, consistently and sensitively. He believed indeed that the material of music itself mirrored this dislocation. For he believed the old tonal centres of music to be caught up in an inevitable process of weakening to extinction.

Schönberg wished to give order to the anarchy of these centreless musical notes, that is the twelve equal semitones of the equal tempered octave, by arranging them for the purposes of each composition into a subjectively chosen alphabetical row, which is to be constantly repeated. This is what I would call Schönberg's fundamentalism, absolutely justified for himself but which he failed to justify rationally to the general satisfaction of his peers.

Faced with Schönberg's music as ordered by his system the general listener perceives, or thinks he does, the absence of a tone *centre*, but does not perceive the organization due to the tone *row*. (Hence, of course, the sense of frustration.) But if he does not perceive Schönberg's own organization, what in fact does he perceive? And there by a long detour we reach the centre of Ehrenzweig's book: the nature of aesthetic perception. What did past ages perceive in art, and what do we now perceive in the difficult works called modern art?

I can usefully quote here two sentences from the summary of Ehrenzweig's book as it appears on the inside of the dust cover:

It is a familiar fact that new art matures into a mellow historical style in the course of a few generations, and that music which at first seems to have no harmonic sound yields later the qualities it had apparently lacked. The author suggests that this gradual transformation is not due to a belated understanding on the part of the public, but to certain dynamic changes in its perception (that is the public's perception) which projects more and more articulate order into the original half-articulate structure created by the artist.

This is indeed what the book is about. It uses psychoanalytical disciplines to examine the question of why we all have an inexhaustible psychological need to project aesthetic order upon everything presented to us; I mean offered to us as being potentially, even if at first only half-articulately, an aesthetic experience. The book examines what the artist is up to when he produces a half-articulate structure for the public later to re-order, instead of a fully-articulate structure calling for no such public ordering.

Ehrenzweig holds that a fully-articulate structure appeals immediately only to the sharp perceptions of our conscious mind, which corrects any and every sense impression in order to perceive the only thing it can perceive – a shape, a form, a defined object, or what the psychologists call a Gestalt. The scientific discussion of what exactly are the corrections and distortions and additions and suppressions made by the mind in its necessity for form, is truly fascinating. The distinction then made between the mind's basic need for form and the more special need for aesthetic articulation is very subtle, though more problematic. But Ehrenzweig is probably right when he suggests that the artist is forced to abandon the fully-articulated structure just because he is afraid this will be immediately perceived by the current conventional conscious public mind. For he realizes that only by frustrating and refusing this conscious perception is the way open to perception by the peripheral confused attention of the unconscious mind. Ehrenzweig holds that – and I must now use this jargon without timidity – the riches of our plastic sensibilities all come from this unconscious source, to be refined only later by our conscious Gestalt-forming tendencies, Or as Yeats said of the latter activity:

Measurement began our might.

But as soon as measurement has done its work and the public has re-projected, as it must if the work of art is to live, aesthetic order on to previous disorder, then the next artist has already broken the ruler, twisted the compass, and is looking once more through the wrong end of the telescope.

But what Ehrenzweig does not discuss is the more mysterious question that lies behind this: what is the relation, if any, between the kind of half-articulate structure an artist presents to the public at any time as a new work of art, and the actual half-articulate structure which the public does in historical fact re-order? And I must say it *seems* that when one embarks on that question one is leaving the Freudian sea for the Jungian ocean. But in an analogous sense it is part of that exciting book, Edmund Wilson's *To the Finland Station*, which discusses the question: what is happening to you and to History, with a capital H, when *you* think you are History? We know the outcome, because the train from Finland really drew into the station, and Lenin with the bouquet of flowers 'which harmonized rather badly with his whole figure' turned from an official to the crowd beyond. But what we do not know is the substantial relation between the eventual Bayreuth and the young Wagner rejecting the fully-articulate structures of the conventional opera of his time. And further, now that we seem to be in a period of almost total rejection, with numberless young Wagners without the ghost of a chance of an eventual Bayreuth or Valhalla, is it just an accident who, in Samuel Butler's phrase, 'gets squatting rights on the public's ear'?

That this really is a difficult artistic period is a commonplace. Professor Worringer made a bit more precise what we mean, by distinguishing two absolute poles of artistic social behaviour: one based on the absolute right of the consumer, the other on the absolute right of the producer. Within these terms one can say that as the state, or officialdom, whether bourgeois or soviet, or what you will, has tended towards the absolute right of the consumer, the general reaction of all artists of any significance has been to stand fast on an inalienable right of the producer. But Worringer believes that this struggle is not equally apparent or evident in all the arts. He holds that the real point of acute dispute is within the visual arts, because here the distortion of the so-called natural objects is crystal clear to the conscious perception and signally offensive.

Of course, it is not objects in nature alone. In fact Ehrenzweig shows clearly enough that the Gestalt, that is the form, we apprehend is never the natural object which the eye receives as an image on the retina. The mind corrects the sense data in order to present the Gestalt (whether in nature or of an artifact) and the Gestalt alone as the object of conscious apprehension. While the *eye* of a person entering a dining-room with a long table set with plates in diminishing perspective receives in fact the strictly visual impression of a set of circular objects becoming progressively elliptical in the vanishing perspective, the conscious *mind* thinks the eye perceives a dinner table set with round plates, and round plates only. So when Cézanne first paints the table as seen by the eye alone, and offers his canvas to us then as though the mind saw the table like this, then Cézanne is being truer to what the eye really sees just in order to baffle the formative tendencies of our conscious mind, because he wants us to be forced to apprehend some other things, some other relationships; and when we do eventually satisfy our psychological need to see the apparently distorted objects of the picture in a new order, a new set of relations, it is an aesthetic one which is perceived and an aesthetic plum we enjoy.

The same argument goes for the impressionist attempt to paint the physically accurate effects of light, or for the earlier discoveries of perspective. And in an amusing anecdote about Dürer, Ehrenzweig shows once for all how impossible it is to make any sense of the artistic movement from medieval painting through so-called naturalist painting to the present, by any appeal solely to the external objects which the painter represents. For Dürer wanted to go to the extreme in this matter and to make corrections even for the perspective which operates between the centre and the edge of any very large picture; that is, to allow not only for the perspective of the objects represented, but also for the perspective of the canvas itself, just because a spectator must stand away somewhere from the picture and in one place at a time. So Dürer set up a huge plate of glass in the shape of a picture, and tried to paint on the glass exactly what he saw behind in his studio; so that on looking from a certain place at the picture on the glass you would see, so far as you knew, the studio behind. The results were very odd! Just about as odd probably as real human figures looked walking backward and forward in the so-called realistic perspective scenery of the late Renaissance stage. For the perspective of the painted scene could give the hallucination of a distance on the stage many times greater than that of the actual stage upon which the living actors are forced to move. But to worry about such a matter is not to know the aesthetic experience at all.

To use the psychoanalytical disciplines as Ehrenzweig does to examine the aesthetic experience, is really to be taken behind the scenes and to see the matter from the wings and the flies and the trapdoors.

I have never experienced the complete incomprehension with respect to my music that Schönberg suffered. His is an extreme case and the process of reaching aesthetic enjoyment through re-ordering, in the sense of Dr Ehrenzweig's book, is unduly protracted. Schönbergians are certain that this protracted process will eventually be accomplished; Schönberg will be publicly accepted. But some at least of the public if not indeed musicians feel this to be the petitio principii. *If one cannot re-order the apparently meaningless music so that it can be enjoyed as we enjoy other comparable music, then how can one yet know that in time this meaningless music will eventually seem clear? I mentioned this matter in this last paper, but I have no certain idea. I think those who are able make an* a priori *judgement, a kind of prophecy, based on some intuitive apprehension, which enables them to imagine the music in its clear statement, such as the composer has done in the process of creation. Presumably this intuitive sense is one of the gifts of a good critic.*

Because music has to be re-created in performance, then it is common sense to suppose that problems of execution make a critic's initial and intuitive judgement more fallible. For instance, when A Child of Our Time *was first performed it appeared stranger than it does now. It was never rejected, but it was much criticized; and among other things for its orchestration. Recently one of the younger English critics apologized to me, with a generosity unusual in a critic, for having condemned the orchestration at the start, whereas now he felt it to be appropriate and imaginative. He was speaking, as he knew, for many others.*

In such a simple case of revision of critical judgement in music, we may reasonably suppose that the critic is only reacting to better conditions of performance. Yet I think that something must also be set down to the passage of time. For my experience of much better first performances than that of A Child of Our Time *is that the real relations of the tones escape somehow out of the net of even the most notationally accurate* première. *I mean by 'real relations' just those particular relations which are appropriate for this one piece of music. (They will include the blending of instruments, the orchestration.) If the real relations are operating then the thousands of notes will seem to cohere. All the right notes can be played at a first performance and yet they do not appear to cohere – except of course to those few gifted with prophetic imaginative intuition. For the rest it is a question of time and repetition. Even a second performance is already easier. If the work is good (and this remains the* petitio principii*) then the passage of time helps both performers and listeners alike. Whether the passage of time always operates according to Dr Ehrenzweig's theory is disputable. Ehrenzweig speaks a lot of Schönberg, and I can believe that Schönberg is a better case for the theory than I shall ever be.*

The prejudices which inhibit acceptance are not always recondite. The critic who said of A Child of Our Time *that not even genius could make incitement to political murder palatable, seems so extremely stupid now that he is well forgotten. Yet he was an intelligent critic about music that he knew and loved. He spoke for those who resented being moved in the way* A Child of Our Time *must move an audience if the music is to be itself. Were he still living it would be interesting to have had his recantation, or not, after the due passage of time. I think he would have gone along with the majority. The political accidents behind the story of the pieces have passed into history, leaving the way clear for a younger generation to accept* A Child of Our Time *in the direct way they do.*

Lastly I mention those criticisms pointed at my using negro spirituals within such an apparently sophisticated score. Here I think we can see that the original incompatibility of emotionally complex composed music and popularly derived simple melody, if set side by side without mediation, lead critics into a prejudice at a first hearing, which could not be overcome until the mediatory process (akin to Ehrenzweig's re-ordering) is understood. It is perhaps analogous to the shocks people first had at being presented with the mixture of sophisticated and popular in the poems of W. H. Auden. The passage of time has uncovered the poetic connections. So it has done with the musical connections of A Child of Our Time. *The transitions from composed music to the settings of the spirituals are accepted now as one of the achievements of the piece.*

I have drawn attention to this popular, or simple, side of A Child of Our Time, *because simplicity can be rejected as well as complication. Generally we think of initial critical misunderstanding and rejection as arising from the new work's extreme difficulty. But if extreme difficulty, whether of style or execution, becomes in snob circles over-valued as such, then a special prejudice can arise, within the general difficulty the public has with modern art, against the simple. This is certainly a danger. I can imagine a very young man's work nowadays suffering the usual depreciation and rejection because of a fresh simplicity.*

The answer to : What in new art will in fact *survive ? is, despite Dr Ehrenzweig, anyone's guess. Since there is no formula for the perception of value in new work, the* petitio principii *of what is good in what is currently offered remains.*

9 A Composer and His Public

The radio has turned out to be one of the most practical aids to the dissemination of new music. Where radio executives have assumed a social responsibility to any degree the results have been nothing but good. The principle of the Third Programme, that a wave-length should exist to provide for cultural minorities in the good sense, was probably the biggest step forward. Hence its imitation on the continent; and hence the feeling of protest and dejection when the B.B.C. Third Programme was unilaterally curtailed. Discs of new music are possibly an even greater practical aid, but the recording companies have not assumed any comparable social responsibility.

The radio has also tried to build bridges between artist and public through the spoken word. There is little doubt that the impact of a living personality through the radio helps in more ways than the limited content of what the composer, or other artist says. 'A Composer's Point of View' was part of a series of talks for the B.B.C. under the general title of 'The Artist and His Public'. All the different arts were represented.

Whether responsible television will prove an even better aid to the dissemination of new art is yet to be known. On the face of it one imagines that television reproduces visual arts better than music. But the television interview may sharpen and widen the impact of a living personality beyond anything sound radio can do. This kind of secondary contact between artist and public is not to be dismissed as unworthy.

It is an act of faith to address an invisible audience. Is that faith anything to do with the much deeper faith, the faith in the ultimate virtue of the creative act, which a composer must have to write music at all in this time? What, in this matter of the Composer and His Public, has been there always and what is new?

We have been for centuries used to receiving letters through the post, sheets of lines and blobs on paper, which when taken out of the envelope tell us things, and often in such a tone that we can imagine the loved (or hated) voice speaking out of the ink. This is the primeval miracle of any communication at a distance. So living a thing indeed is a letter that when Nora's husband in *A Doll's House* tears up the letter that should have reached his wife, we feel that something has been done much more destructive than any burning of waste paper, for the letter is a symbol of communication and to prevent it from reaching its destination is to do the two people concerned an injury.

Or, to be more up to date, we can think of Menotti's operetta, *The Telephone*, where a young man in a hurry has difficulty in proposing to his girl because she is so constantly interrupted by telephone conversations. The young man only succeeds when he has the sense to go out to the nearest call-box and put his proposal by telephone. The satire turns all upon the possibility that in modern society we value communication at a distance too much. But to be more up to date still and to consider the techniques of communication by radio, is to be forced to admit the extraordinary immediacy of the method, particularly of television. There is a dash of the fabulous about communicating instantly as though the space between Broadcasting House and one's home were annihilated. In so far as communication is part of art, surely the new conditions of communicating will affect to some extent all the various arts? Particularly, perhaps, the art of music, because music depends only on the immediate perception of sound, and not, as in literature, on sight, or the reading of words (as though we had been sent a very long letter).

I used to think, before radio came, that the song recital was tending to die out as a means of making music before a public; that it had had its day, and that with the decline of the recital would come the death of the song (as a musical form). But radio suits the genius of the song recital very well, and the sound in our home can be intimate and delightful. Remembering what I once thought, I am gratified now to realize that I have since written works for voice and piano, and hope to write more. We respond to the new means to hand.

Again, a young composer must have always wondered just where his public was to be found. But in our day, when there seems a kind of law that the more seriously a composer applies himself to his art, the less public he can have at all, the serious young composer may come to feel he cannot start anywhere; that his public must remain ever non-existent. Yet the truth of the matter may be that his public is just of ones and twos, those few folk really interested in new things; and here it is that through the radio, if his music can once be played, his public of ones and twos can be assembled, so to speak, without assembling. This is in fact what does happen. Most new music begins its real public life on the radio.

Nevertheless radio has not changed our musical social life so radically that we go no more to concerts, because radio cannot reproduce all the real thing. I remember in the old Queen's Hall the young Furtwängler conducting the Beethoven Ninth, his back properly turned to the packed audience, but this same back receiving all the while those invisible waves of absorption and attention which a great public gives to great music. Psychological conditions of performance were then magically made which are virtually impossible in a studio. These are still the dream conditions of the composer, I think. This is his public in the flesh. This is where he wants to be played and understood. This still means more to him than radio. As Joyce Cary has said, this public is classless; or perhaps, it is the class of all the lovers of music. It is never all the human race, but only some. And despite our new methods of communication by radio and television, the big public that wants to hear music in concert halls and see opera in theatres, is still our idea of the Musical Public.

If, then, I as a composer want to have a living relation with this big public which goes to concerts and operas, I must consider how to get round, or mitigate the incidence of, that law which seems to say that the more serious a modern composer is, the less able he is to speak to anything beyond a coterie. Obviously I cannot alone, by myself, remove the wide and enduring disrelation between all new art and the big public. That there is such a disrelation now cannot be denied.

Let us now call the composer and the public the producer and the consumer, because that is the relation between artist and public; but this relation is not so immediate and therefore so obvious in the arts as in commerce. If it were so, there would be the same demand for the latest music as there is for the latest house furnishing, or for television. But, as we all know, the popular demand for television is part of the general preoccupation of our society with gadgets, and with speed, and with mechanical progress; with a gay time; and not really a popular demand for art communicated through television. The huge public for radio, or for films, or for sport, or whatever, holds the demand of the consumer to be paramount; and in so far as this public is our government and state, then the modern bureaucratic machines also hold to this one hundred per cent consumer point of view. Seen from this point of view the composer is only a servant of the big public, whose taste he must accept or starve.

Put bluntly in this way, it does sound rather excessive. We all know that the big public is extremely conservative, and willing to ring the changes on a few beloved works till the end of time, and that our concert life, through the taste of this public, suffers from a kind of inertia of sensibility, that seems to want no musical experience whatever beyond what it already knows. When this taste is indeed the national taste, the art of the nation certainly dies. But the creative artist is passionately determined that it shall not die. In fact totalitarian societies which are pathetically con- formist and afraid of the new, have had to stamp him out. They are afraid – even of the struggling composer with his tiny public; afraid of his passion, of his violence, of his unaccountability. For it is a fact of musical history (and this goes for the other arts as well) that during the last half-century, or even earlier, every major composer has at the outset found the taste of the big public and its consumer point of view unacceptable. And in counterblast there has never been a period where so many manifestoes have been issued demanding the absolute freedom of the artist to create what he likes, so many proclamations of a one hundred per cent producer point of view.

I think of Bartók, who was certainly a victim of this division. To the end of his life he had relations only with those small, select groups which side with the artists against the big public. He died in poverty. It does not matter whether his extreme works are banned in his homeland, that is in Hungary, or only seldom played over here. The issue is the same. He stands, a terrifying example of the maximum disrelation between a great creative energy and the mass public.

This brings us to my next point; which arises out of the fact that while patronage might have kept Bartók from under-nourishment (he received in fact a great deal of patronage during his life), no amount of patronage could bring his extreme producer point of view into relation with the extreme consumer point of view of the big public. The big public and the critics who spoke for it, could hardly deny his creative integrity, but they absolutely rejected his music. No doubt Bartók, for all his courage, was hurt and haunted by this rejection. The last works, which seem so much less dissonant, may have sprung from a deep desire to issue from the profound dilemma of the time by moving somewhat back from his extreme point of view, back towards the conservative public. Or these last works may be the result of a fatigue and loneliness. In no sense can the dilemma be resolved by sneering at the difficult composer on behalf of the big public, or by despising the big public in an attempt to take up cudgels on behalf of the new composer. The dilemma is not a conspiracy but a fact.

Why won't the big public ever come any way to meet artistic integrity when it takes extreme forms of expression? How can a great composer (like Bartók) go forward at all in what looks like a voluntary cul-de-sac? Surely the matter is that the very big public masses together in a kind of dead passion of mediocrity, and that this blanket of mediocrity, whether communist or capitalist, is deeply offended by any living passion of the unusual, the rare, the rich, the exuberant, the heroic, and the aristocratic in art – the art of a poet like Yeats. While it is clear from Yeats's life and writings that in this very passion of defiance an artist can find both material for his art and vigour for his despised activity, we know from other examples, he may starve.

Because, given our present disrelation between artist and public, it is obvious that patronage from one side, from the public, and directed to satisfy the official taste, cannot for that reason be used honestly to satisfy the creative urges of the great artist. In truth it is an illusion to think it really ever has been. When Haydn lived at Esterhazy under the direct patronage of his Prince, he composed music that satisfied the energies of his creative life (that is, of himself as producer) as well as satisfying the needs of the musical entertainment for the Court (that is, of the consumers). Principally he could do this because his public was not in any sense a mass public, but a select public of cultivated people as interested in the newest music as in the newest house furnishings. There was then no dilemma.

But in the case of Bach, whose patrons were the Municipality and the Lutheran Church Authorities, there was dilemma. Bach was accused of being difficult and obscure, as well as of being somewhat old fashioned. His creative gifts were not fully absorbed by the consumers who were his public and his patrons. The modern composer's dilemma is only Bach's dilemma writ large. His hope is that his works will nevertheless survive, as Bach's have survived, whether they can be absorbed by the musical consumer of his time or not. In the end the question of value and survival seems independent of whether the conditions of production are like Haydn's or like Bach's. What alone has immortality, if there is to be such in any period, is the work of art born from just this living passion of creation. The dead passion of mediocrity may kill the living artist and the nation's art; but it cannot project its own deadness beyond its own death.

Having, then, outlined the general conditions as I see them, where do I stand myself? I must now affirm simply that I know of no other absolute in this matter than the power of such creative energies as I possess; that I look, therefore, at public and patronage through the eyes of a dedicated person, who must do what he has to do, whether the issue is acceptable or not; that my passion is to project into our mean world music which is rich and generous; that I hope I reject mediocrity as intensely as it rejects me. But these violent words spring from the vigour and passion of my artistic life, not from any violence in my person.

Indeed, when the creative energies are not fully used up in bringing to expression what I need most deeply to say, then I have enjoyed doing works for specific commissions – works like the orchestral suite for Prince Charles's birthday. This is relatively simple and unambiguous. I have been less sure when a patron has wanted a work of art. I doubt if this can be done at all except in the sense that the composer is given some financial assistance to his life, while he writes such a work of art as he may; or simply, that the consumer agrees to consume, or to try to consume, exactly what the producer produces. If the patron (whether an individual, or a festival, or the radio) has not understood clearly the reality of this situation, the matter can easily be a cause for distress rather than relief. Patronage by the community at large of creative artists can be easy and unambiguous only in a society where all the artefacts (the gadgets, if you like), the furnishings, the clothes, the songs, the poetry, the images, are lovely and full of power and grace and of a fine and generous tradition. Such a society cannot be found in metropolitan Europe today – nor in Moscow, nor in New York. The beautiful things are rare. And state patronage is too much the mirror of the commonplace culture of our day to be able to alter this situation except occasionally and by accident, as when Le Corbusier builds a whole new city in India.

A contemporary composer realizes all this fairly clearly. Sometimes he offers his talents for commercial gain, sometimes he patronizes himself by obtaining money elsewhere, sometimes he receives public financial help for the work of art he wants to compose. He must accept the last in fear and trembling. There is absolutely no guarantee that, in this present period of cultural anarchy, his patron's taste will agree with his. He must hope it will be reasonably so. But the much deeper hope is a product only of his vigour as an artist, the hope that his work of art will belong in the great tradition.

And what is the great tradition? I would prefer, like Yeats, to call it activation of the Great Memory: that immense reservoir of the human psyche where images age-old and new boil together in some demoniac cauldron; images of the past, shapes of the future; images of vigour for a decadent period, images of calm for one too violent; images of reconciliation for worlds torn by division; images of abounding, generous, exuberant beauty in an age of fear, mediocrity and horror comics.

10 A Time to Recall

When I was a student I submitted entirely to the music of Beethoven. I explored his music so exhaustively that for a long time later on I listened to every other music but his. But as a student I was fascinated by his music and his personality, though I had also a very catholic taste, to which little was foreign. I doubt if in adolescence one can be absorbed by Beethoven and have a real understanding of Mozart. In so far as I have acquired that it has come later. In student days I enjoyed Mozart, as who could not? and heard everything I could. At that period in London we witnessed Mozart operas from cheap and uncomfortable seats in the Old Vic. I can recall the performances even now. But I was then hardly mature enough to savour all his art. I ranged Don Giovanni and The Magic Flute above Figaro and Così fan tutte. Despite all the particular interests I have in the former two due to their special tradition as I have described in 'The Birth of An Opera', I doubt if I would range them now above the latter two. I did not feel called to speak of Mozart's bicentenary as a Mozart scholar. I am deeply interested now in our sense of time. A bicentenary gave an excellent opportunity to think of Mozart's works in his own time and his works in our time. Mr Christopher Holme had asked me a question from which this paper sprang: did Mozart read Werther? The chapter does not really answer all that the question implied, but it tries to find the feel of Mozart's time and to contrast that with the feel of our own time. To come at the feel of our own time led to Chapter 14. The feel of Mozart's time evaded me.

I want to quote a paragraph from a biography of someone born seven years before Mozart:

Whatever the stars may have betokened, this August 1749 was a momentous month to Germany, if only because it gave birth to the man whose influence on his nation has been greater than that of any man since Luther, not excepting Lessing. A momentous month in very momentous times. It was the middle of the eighteenth century: a period when the movement which had culminated in Luther was passing from religion to politics, and freedom of thought was translating itself into liberty of action ... The agitation was still mainly in the higher classes, but it was gradually descending to the lower. A period of deep unrest: big with events that would expand the conceptions of all men, and bewilder some of the wisest.

That quotation is from Lewes's *Life of Goethe*. Lewes, husband of George Eliot, writes not at all as a contemporary of young Goethe and Mozart; but as one looking back to that past from a time when the 'agitation' and 'the deep unrest' had become really violent and profound (though it was to be emotionally held at bay for a while by the dynamic optimism of the Victorians). We ourselves, who know now that we have moved into a period of global agitation and unrest, are inclined in compensation to think of the middle of the eighteenth century as a period of relative calm.

It seems to me that while we might draw attention, as Lewes does, to the latent philosophical and emotional unrest of the eighteenth century if we were starting a biography of Goethe, we would certainly not do so for a biography of Mozart. I think part of our conception of Mozart is formed out of the knowledge that Mozart died young, and died before that latent agitation and unrest had really revealed itself to be the Future. Even in *The Magic Flute*, at the end of Mozart's life, the only opera where philosophical ideas are indeed displayed (and to which Goethe himself wrote a sequel), we cannot find expression of agitation and unrest. We can perhaps find parallels in the prophetic dreams of Rousseau to the ethical idealism of this opera; but we cannot project on to the Queen of the Night the evil and violence that was to come. The figure will not take the charge.

'Whatever the stars may have betokened', writes Lewes, speaking ironically of Goethe's splendid horoscope. More interesting, perhaps, is the strange fact of the prophecy of Nostradamus that 1789 would be a violently decisive year for European history. But no one in the eighteenth century before the 'decisive year' took much account of it, outside the circles of astrology. Certainly Mozart did not. Goethe, indeed, might have done, but more from the side of the mysterious significance of prophecy as such, within the scheme of Time, than from the side of what might happen in 1789 which was to be significant.

There is a poem of Goethe in which these lines occur:

> Und umzuschaffen das Geschaffene,
> Dass sich's nicht zum Starren waffne,
> Wirkt ewiges lebendiges Thun.

which can be roughly translated:

> 'And refashioning the fashioned,
> Lest it stiffen into iron,
> Is work of an endless vital activity.'

That sounds like Beethoven, never like Mozart. There is already present in the Goethe quotation that urge and drive to refashion and invent and overturn, which has gone on till our own day but which is absent in Mozart. Yeats put the matter in another way, but very well. He writes somewhere, in *Estrangement*: 'Our modern poetry is imaginative. It is the poetry of the young. The poetry of the greatest periods is a sustained expression of the appetites and habits. Hence we invent where they exhausted.'

It is clear enough that Mozart is the last great composer who was able to exhaust a conventional artistic diction, and did not have to invent imaginatively in Yeats's sense at all. So it is possible that part of what we want from Mozart is a compensation. We should so like to live in an artistic period where one and a fine style is to be exhausted in a 'sustained expression of the appetites and habits' – but of course Yeats means appetites and habits of a unitary, not a pluralistic, society. We shall not live to see such a period as Mozart's. For although the drive to channel the artistic imagination all into stylistic invention may be slackening, no unitary society is being born. Instead, behind the great façade of Unesco, loom up 'Interrelations of Cultures'. And that means eventually, amongst other things, native African syntax impinging on, say, English syntax; Indian music on European music.

In other words, even though we might hope to see in a reasonably near future a more universally accepted musical, or poetic, style, we still cannot imagine this style exhausted by a 'sustained expression of appetites and habits', in Yeats's sense, because the society into which we are certainly moving is an enormous melting-pot of incredibly different appetites and habits and cultures.

'Those whom the Gods love die young'; meaning that great beauty of form or great heroism of conduct, say Ganymede or Achilles, is often immortalized, taken up into the realm of the undying gods, by the immemorial poignance of an early death. Such an idea does not work for, say, Schubert, where we have a sense of incompletion. It is truer for Mozart, where we have a sense of achieved perfection, made more vivid by an early death. I would not wish him to have lived on to express the turbulence of the French Revolution. And the nineteenth-century views on Mozart's operas, especially those for which da Ponte wrote the librettos, show that the Romantics were well aware in what time Mozart lived; that he was no precursor of theirs; that if he did read *Werther* (published when he was eighteen) it did not draw him into that climate of opinion which was to flower later as Romanticism. Guizot wrote sometime later: 'Aujourd'hui l'homme désire immensément, mais il veut faiblement.' Lewes called this sentence, justly enough, 'an epigraph for *Werther*'. It does not fit the eighteen-year-old Mozart at any point whatsoever. No one willed more strongly than he, no one spent less time in vain nostalgias.

Nor does the sentence fit the hero of *Don Giovanni*, or the lovers of *Così fan tutte*. These operas were a stumbling-block for the Romantics, because the stories did not romanticize love at all. Nor did they enter at any point the world of dreams. I do not personally belittle the Romantics for their opinions of love and 'phantasy'. Their world of dreams was to prove a fabulous cauldron of poetic riches. Nor did the Romantics belittle Mozart, whatever difficulty they had in romanticizing the da Ponte librettos. No less than the arch-romantic E. T. A. Hoffmann changed his third Christian name from Wilhelm to Amadeus! The Romantics were as drawn to Mozart as we are, if differently.

For the Victorians, the da Ponte librettos were another kind of offence. Where the Romantics wanted to romanticize love, the Victorians erected a conventional view of love which attempted or hoped to restrict its expression within the marriage bond. Even though Lewes and George Eliot themselves knew that love can be experienced outside marriage, yet was it not really a kind of Victorian love they experienced? They would not have approved

(I think that is the right word) of the proceedings in *Così fan tutte*, and still less of the hero of *Don Giovanni*. Perhaps 'approved' is not the right word. They would not have felt the situations of these operas as being possible at all. (Lewes, be it remembered, attacked Dickens's novels as being untrue.) They would have thought of the plots as literal, and would have had to moralize them away. Perhaps, indeed, the Victorians, for one reason or another, held Mozart in less esteem than we. But statistics of performances might equally prove that wrong.

Certainly, with the cruder reaction against Victorian morality, that is with the romanticized Don Juanism of the last forty years, we are as far from the spirit of Mozart's *Don Giovanni* as before. Nor do we come any nearer to the classical detachment of Mozart's operas with a man of much finer temper, but who was no moralist in George Eliot's sense – D. H. Lawrence. Perhaps only the late-Victorian George Bernard Shaw, cradled, spiritually, in the Irish eighteenth century, and immune to the romanticism of the Gaelic League, held aloft some kind of Mozartian flame. In 1903 he wrote of Don Juan:

After Molière comes the artist-enchanter, the master of masters, Mozart, who reveals the hero's spirit in magical harmonies, elfin tones, and elate darting rhythms as of summer lightning made audible. Here you have freedom in love and in morality mocking exquisitely at slavery to them, and interesting you, attracting you, tempting you, inexplicably forcing you to range the hero with his enemy the statue on a transcendent plane, leaving the prudish daughter and her priggish lover on a crockery shelf to live piously ever after.

That does not sound at all like our conventional idea of 1903. Indeed, in temper, it seems to reach forward a good half-century. Is it possible that we shall presently rediscover this wonderful prose?

But let us consider a different post-Victorian world: the world of Kafka. Kafka writes:

They describe the poet as a wonderful big man, whose feet are indeed on earth, but whose head disappears in the clouds. That is of course a quite common and conventional lower-middle-class picture. It is an illusion of hidden desires, and has nothing whatever to do with reality. In reality the poet is much smaller and weaker than the average man of society. So he feels the weight of our earthly existence much more strongly and intensively than they do. His song is for himself personally only a shriek. Art is for the artist sorrow, through which he frees himself for a further sorrow.

That somewhat exaggerated statement has, all the same, real experiences behind it, and is sustained by the real discoveries of depth psychology. This psychology made a scientific study of (and I had better use the scientific term) infantile sexuality; that is, of the unconscious consequences of the libido's frustrations during childhood. Then the question was asked: how did the grown-up and normally healthy man sublimate these unmentionable and repressed desires? And how could the mentally sick of them be healed? To Freud, the artist appears just as much as the rest a prey to these unconscious forces. Indeed, he suggests that the artist suffers more from these repressed conflicts than the ordinary person; but, in compensation, that the artist can achieve a sublimation of them, instead of a neurosis, through his art.

Mozart's childhood under his tyrannical father would seem to be a textbook opportunity for the Oedipus complex. Nor do I doubt but that it existed. And in some sense (though perhaps it is not quite so exact a sense as the psychologists think) Mozart's art is his sublimation. But the interesting thing is that we cannot gain any insight into Mozart's unconscious conflicts from his music, in the way that Kafka's prose seems actually made out of his neurosis, and Schönberg's music very possibly out of his. Clearly the archetypal situations affected the eighteenth-century artist as much as they do all of us. But for the expression of them in an art of personal predicament, that mysterious thing, the Time, was not ripe. We must admit, therefore, that however much we may feel we have now a special relation to Mozart, we are not the Man, with a capital M, whom Mozart had in mind when he composed. Nor are we any more his apparent antithesis, the heroic revolutionary Man, or Woman of *Fidelio* and the Ninth Symphony. We certainly have been for quite a long time Kafka's Man; that is the Man for whom God is the guilt-ridden neurosis. And if, schooled by Sartre, we are now to wear this God like a flower in the button-hole, are we yet any kind of Man to whom a modern Mozart, were there one, might speak?

Only a little while ago there appeared an article in a national newspaper called 'The New Puritans'. The article sought to draw some conclusions about the coming generation from the examination papers of a large group of university scholarships. Leaving the scientists aside and considering the answers only of the arts specialists, the article suggests that these answers 'imply that these eighteen-year-olds are not sentimental, they would like to be taken as hard-headed'. The fairy tales of the German romantics are dismissed as sickly. Music exists in its highest form as pure abstraction, without the aid of programme notes or 'pretty pictures'; Stravinsky is right: 'music can express absolutely nothing.' The didactic function of drama is emphasized; the exploration of the emotions is played down or treated as 'psychological'.

I find that interesting and revealing. With such a temper Mozart should be justly appreciated, and perhaps *The Rake's Progress* even more. Yet I do not myself believe that the real revolution of our time, the discovery and invention of the Unconscious, has by any means run its course. Let me quote the following:

For example, since 3 is a male number and 4 a female number, the sum of the two expresses the complete being, that is a double being, partaking of both sexes (every being having two souls, one of either sex). This indicates that the true unit is composed of a couple. But this couple, although complete, cannot be perfect unless it possesses the primordial Word, the promoter and Monitor of Creation; and this Word is represented by the figure 8, that is the couple seven with the addition of the One.

That sounds like Professor Jung discussing the value of alchemy to modern dream interpretation. But it is not so. It comes from a scientific essay published by Unesco on *The Problem of Negro Culture*, and it appeared first in 1953. To read all the other essays of this Unesco publication is to put the examination papers of the Cambridge candidates into perspective.

Yet the strangest fact of all is that the religious ideas of the Dogon Negroes could have appeared easily in *The Magic Flute*.

11 An Irish Basset-Horn

Over a number of years I have had an illuminating experience watching the maturation of a young conductor. The more he matured and the further he became absorbed in the functions on his side of the art of music, the less we were able to share any musical experiences at all. I became aware more sharply than I ever knew before that by now I only listen to music with attention to its content and its form. I judge these things all the time; not in any true sense objectively, but with a searching ear for their aid in my own compositional problems. It is long indeed since I was caught up into a piece of music through the perfection of its performance. Even Toscanini's Brahms Two performed last in London superbly, as I well realized at the time, meant infinitely more because after six years of hard work on operatic composition I was weary of my own descriptive music and thirsting for symphonic fountains. The young conductor on the other hand was engrossed by the problems of performance, measuring Toscanini against his other gods, Monteux, Karajan. Although we both listened to the same symphony at the same performance our experiences were apparently quite different.

What would a critic have experienced? An interesting question; and which must be partially answerable on the same lines. Obviously if the composer experiences only those things pertaining to his own subjective condition as a composer, and the conductor only those things pertaining to performance as an art within the art, then the critic experiences those things which enable him to make the critical judgement he needs to. He will observe performance, if he is to criticize the performers, and he will observe form and content if he is to criticize the work. Looked at in this way he should be quite a considerable person.

I have already spoken in Chapter 8 of my feeling that a first performance of a new work can hardly ever present an immediately coherent image for appreciation. I suggested that the critic needs *therefore a prophetically intuitive sixth sense which can give him immediately the material for critical judgement denied to the general public. I think this gift is rare. Knowing this gift is rare the practising composer expects little help from the mass of criticisms he receives. For my own part I rarely read them. This is not merely a self-protective gesture against being hurt, for one can't be sure one will not be flattered, but because I find the criticisms hardly addressed to me at all. The known critics have such familiar attitudes it takes very little to guess correctly in advance what they will say. Mr So-and-So is an embattled defender of The Establishment, while Mr Other-So wants to be thought avant garde. So-and-So, under the impact of a staggering performance by a foreign orchestra, can revise his opinion of a work of mine sufficiently to affirm it worthy to stand beside Elgar or Vaughan Williams. Other-So remains unconvinced. If the composer is to write at all he must do so in despite of critics.*

Yet a composer gladly accepts criticism that can bring him to see faults or tendencies which he has not clearly seen for himself. Such criticism is probably not public criticism at all. I have found that it needs quite a long breakdown of critical periphrasis into technical fact before the criticism can reveal the value it may have. This can only be done verbally. What one misses from written English musical criticisms is that percipience and illumination, the ordering of the new particular within the generality, whether traditional or of the day, which one gets from good English literary criticism. This is in part also the cry of Bernard Shaw. It may be that the conditions of reviewing performances at concerts are so different from reviewing books at home, that our cry is vain. But Shaw certainly managed on the spot musical criticism, which is often penetrating in its percipience.

I never met Shaw, unluckily. The nearest I came to it was seeing his back withdrawing into a taxi after he had lunched with Samuel Butler's biographer, Festing Jones, with whom I as a very young man was going to tea. Jones told me that Shaw met Butler a few times and that they talked music. All went well until Shaw mentioned Wagner, then it was all over; Butler could not stand Wagner. The curious thing is that Butler, who hated stuffiness and academicism in literature and painting, spent a lot of time learning composition in order to write music like Handel. This was an endearing trait, but gave him no insight into the world of living music at all. Shaw was as rebellious as Butler, but his insight into the musical world around him was signally acute. I doubt he ever tried to compose at all. Shaw was always the professional, Butler often the amateur.

George Bernard Shaw had a good ear for music and a superb ear for language; that is, for English prose. In his young manhood he incessantly educated, polished and trained his musical and literary ears; so when in his thirties he became musical critic of *The Star* and later of *The World* he already knew how to use his one ear to understand and criticize all the music he heard, and how to use his other ear to express his criticisms in whatever literary manner he chose. He could be witty, elegant, paradoxical, profound, didactic at will. He did not wish to be dull, and never was.

Shaw describes how his political articles so alarmed the editor of *The Star*, when offered to him, that T. P. O'Connor, who had just founded the paper, would have perforce dismissed him from his staff, if Shaw had not suggested a weekly '*feuilleton* on music'. O'Connor, it appears, was glad to get rid of Shaw's politics on these terms, but stipulated that 'musical criticism being known to him only as unreadable and unintelligible jargon' Shaw should, 'for God's sake, not write about Bach in B Minor'. Shaw was quite alive to that danger and had only made the proposal because, as he says: 'I believed I could make musical criticism readable even by the deaf.'

With his racy Irish-English style Shaw certainly saw to it that his weekly *feuilleton* was readable. But it brought him a good deal of trouble with the musicians. He was not even writing for *The Star*, as he was to do later for *The World*, under his own name, but had decided to dramatize himself as 'a fantastic personality with something like a foreign title'. He chose Corno di Bassetto for the name and title and for two years he 'sparkled every week in *The Star* under this ridiculous name', but 'in a manner so absolutely unlike the conventional musical criticism of the time', that his *feuilleton* was thought to be a joke, and his knowledge of music negligible. In fact his musical knowledge was extraordinary, and his judgement valuable if unorthodox.

Shaw detested musical journalese and set out to kill it. He never wrote it himself but occasionally he pilloried it. For example, he quotes the following from a set of essays on *Form and Design in Music*, where a Mr Heathcote Statham 'parses' Mozart's G Minor

Symphony 'in the most edifying academic manner'. Statham seems to have written the following:

The principal subject, hitherto, only heard in the treble, is transferred to the bass (Ex. 28), the violins playing a new counterpoint to it instead of the original mere accompaniment figure of the first part. Then the parts are reversed, the violins taking the subject and the basses the counterpoint figure, and so on till we come to a close on the dominant of D minor, a nearly related key (commencement of Ex. 29), and then comes the passage by which we return to the first subject in its original form and key.

I have quoted all the passage as Shaw quotes it, because it has a nice rounded balance of its own kind. And because Shaw, basing his ridicule on our acknowledged acceptance of the futility of such analysis, if transferred to poetry, composes a complementary period, which shall represent what he calls his 'celebrated "analysis" of Hamlet's soliloquy on suicide, in the same scientific style'. Mimicking Statham, Shaw writes:

Shakespeare, dispensing with the customary exordium, announces his subject at once in the infinitive, in which mood it is presently repeated after a short connecting passage in which, brief as it is, we recognize the alternative and negative forms on which so much of the significance of repetition depends. Here we reach a colon; and a pointed pository phrase, in which the accent falls decisively on the relative pronoun, brings us to the first full stop.

Despite such efforts at ridicule we must admit, I am afraid, that Shaw never succeeded in convincing musical critics of the inanity of 'parsing'. If he had lived to be a hundred he would have found present examples not only in writings about the classics (virtually word for word what Statham wrote), but also in writings by critics of such an up-to-date phenomenon as the twelve-note school. For it is lamentably true that music composed within the twelve-note system lends itself readily to 'parsing', and that few critics, or musicologists, when writing of this music, can resist the temptation to palm off on us a pseudo-scientific analysis in lieu of an aesthetic judgement. The aesthetic judgement in music, as Shaw tirelessly expounds, can only be based on what the sensibility perceives of what the ear hears. He believed indeed that conditions of performance are always such that critics must resort to the

scores to correct the textual and interpretative errors of performance. But the aim of the critic in public is judgement not analysis.
Aesthetic judgement, as of the twelve-note music, for example, is
unfortunately often difficult, while analysis is fatally easy. Yet
judgement we must have (if only the judgement of time) while
analysis is only make-believe and very boring.

Now Shaw tried to drive home the point that we never dream
of stomaching literary criticism so otiose and false; because,
according to him, literature, drama and poetry had never been
academized in England in the same way as music and painting.
Whether he got this opinion from Samuel Butler, or whether, as
I guess, it was natural to them both, Shaw and Butler never
wavered in their view that literature and drama and poetry are
everywhere in England sustained and judged by what our
sensibilities perceive directly when we read or go to the theatre;
while in painting, sculpture and music it tends to be the reverse.
We do not allow our sensibilities to perceive directly in these arts.
We go to exhibitions and concerts with labels in our eyes and ears.
Emotionally charged words, such as abstraction and dissonance,
distort our sensibilities. Therefore we do not perceive. And the
public critics of these arts, rarely rising above the general in-
capacity, gurgitate out their flaccid and depressing English style,
devoid of any elegance, wit, profundity, or perception – those
virtues, which as Shaw and Butler knew, can come only from the
real, if personal, judgement of an active sensibility.

But another consequence arose from Corno di Bassetto, who
was to become a dramatist: his intense dislike of what he called
English Festival Oratorio. His fierce criticisms of oratorios were
fed from two fires. He believed on the one hand that musical
academicism not only stifled natural critical judgement, but stifled
also original composition; so that composers of natural gifts were
endlessly led astray down the path of Handelian and Mendel-
ssohnian imitation. On the other hand his literary appreciation of
the Bible was insulted by the glaring discrepancy between the
beautiful, virile, and often violently barbaric text, and the
academic, sentimental, and bloodless music to which it was set.

One might say that the matter came to its hottest head over
Parry's 'Job'. Shaw had avoided the *première* by not attending the
Three Choirs Festival of 1892. But in May 1893, by design or
accident, he 'unluckily went . . . to the concert of the Middlesex

Choral Union, where the first thing that happened was the appearance of Dr Parry amid the burst of affectionate applause that always greets him.' Shaw pretends to be unaware of what was in store until, 'up got Mr Bantock Pierpoint, and sang, without a word of warning, "There was a man in the land of Uz whose name was Job".' Then, Shaw writes: 'I knew I was in for it; and now I must do my duty.'

One is sorry for Parry coming under the lash of Shaw's whip; but one is also sorry for Shaw. It is never pleasant for a critic to do his duty concerning a contemporary idol both of academic taste and the amateur public. Shaw did his duty in the following words:

I take 'Job' to be, on the whole, the most utter failure ever achieved by a thoroughly respectworthy musician. There is not one bar in it that comes within 50,000 miles of the tamest line in the poem. This is the naked, unexaggerated truth. Is anybody surprised at it? Here, on the one hand, is an ancient poem which has lived from civilization to civilization, and has been translated into an English version of haunting beauty and nobility of style, offering to the musician a subject which would have taxed to the utmost the highest powers of Bach, Handel, Mozart, or Wagner. Here on the other hand is not Bach nor Handel nor Mozart nor Beethoven nor Wagner, not even Mendelssohn or Schumann, but ...

Perhaps it is a little like using a sledge-hammer to crack a nut. Parry's 'Job' has gone the way of all such works, for the one certain thing about academic mediocrity is that it cannot outlast its generation. But Shaw was bent on ridding English musical life of pedantry and provincialism. He would acknowledge no English composer as a master till Elgar came. And of course he was right. Yet Shaw never despised Savoy Opera and Sir Arthur Sullivan. He had unstinted praise for what intelligent management like that of D'Oyly Carte could do with such artists of genius as Gilbert and Sullivan, and with a professionally trained and permanent company. He as ceaselessly attacked Augustus Harris for his failure to run Covent Garden on such a basis, though he admitted that it could never be accomplished without state aid. He regarded Covent Garden as anarchic and anachronistic, everything depending solely on the whims of star singers like the de Reszkes. No artistic policy was possible, the repertoire was haphazard, stage management, or as we would say, production, non-existent; there was no permanent company and the only two performances of *The Ring* during the twenty years of the Harris regime were the work of a visiting German company – singers, conductor, orchestra, and all.

We have gone a long way since then. Our serious musical critics never cover the present-day musicals as Shaw covered Victorian comic opera. But Covent Garden and Sadler's Wells, as we know them, are something Shaw only dreamed of, though he was prophet enough to know they would come. There is too much music nowadays in London for a critic in one person to cover both opera and musical; yet it is refreshing to come across Shaw's voracity and catholicity. He had an appetite for everything, from Bayreuth to the village concert in Penalt, Mon. But he refused to get his values wrong. Parry was not Handel, as Sullivan was not Wagner. He makes one curious statement, that he considered the only composer who might have written an English *Meistersinger*, had his life-span been transposed, was Henry Purcell. In this he was remarkably perceptive of later taste, just as he was in his belief, apropos of the *première* of *Falstaff*, that there would come a Verdi revival when the Wagner craze had run its course.

Dramatic music interested Shaw especially. His favourite composer was Mozart; Mozart of *The Magic Flute*, and *Don Giovanni*. Yet he appreciated Mozart for other and more particularly eighteenth-century virtues. As he writes:

In the ardent regions where all the rest are excited and vehement, Mozart alone is completely self-possessed: where they are clutching their bars with a grip of iron and forging them with Cyclopean blows, his gentleness of touch never deserts him: he is considerate, economical, practical, under the same pressure of inspiration that throws your Titan into convulsions.

But Shaw appreciated the Titans, too; at least those who, like Beethoven and Wagner, composed their pieces out of a developed dramatic instinct. He had much less sympathy with a lyrical genius like Schubert, and he failed utterly to see what there was in Brahms. He disliked Brahms because he regarded him as the arch-model for all those late-nineteenth-century English composers who believed that the dramatically conceived sonata forms of Beethoven could be brought to life again by pouring into them lyrical and descriptive music, as we pour blancmange into a mould.

Shaw had an intense Augustan dislike for the confusion of genres. He disliked it in the theatre, and he disliked it in music. And he felt he detected it in the quartets and quintets and concertos and symphonies of the Mackenzies and Macfarrens, the Cowens, the Parrys, the Stanfords. He always wrote of Stanford as Professor Stanford, to underline the nature of his distaste. And he held that there was an inevitable war waged between Professor Stanford of the Royal College of Music rules of composition *à la* Brahms, and plain Charley Stanford of the Irish folk-song settings. Shaw discusses the matter at some length in his review of Stanford's Irish Symphony, beginning: 'The success of Professor Stanford's Irish Symphony last Thursday was, from the Philharmonic point of view, somewhat scandalous. The spectacle of a university professor "going Fantee" is indecorous, though to me personally it is delightful.'

Shaw then goes on to examine the nature of the Irishman's relation to England, before he turns to the matter of folk-song, or 'folky' elements being introduced into concerted music. He talks of Mendelssohn of the 'Scotch' Symphony, of Liszt, Bruch, Dvořák, and Brahms, as examples of composers using folky elements of other races than their own, until he comes to examples using folk-song of their own race, saying:

But in recent cases where the so-called folk-music is written by a composer of the folk himself, and especially of the Celtic folk, with its intense national sentiment, there is the most violent repugnance between the popular music and the sonata form. The Irish Symphony, composed by an Irishman, is a record of fearful conflict between the aboriginal Celt and the Professor.

Being half an aboriginal Celt myself I must admit I find this very refreshing. Being also a composer, I can appreciate this further Shavian observation:

The essence of the sonata form is the development of themes; and even in a rondo a theme that will not develop will not fit the form. Now the greatest folk-songs are final developments in themselves: they cannot be carried any further. You cannot develop 'God Save the Queen', though you may, like Beethoven, write some interesting but retrograde variations on it. Neither can you develop 'Let Erin Remember'.

That was written in 1893 and was still being echoed by Constant Lambert in 1934; for concerted music influenced by folk-song did not reach its greatest example until the works of Bartók. But the period is now definitely closed.

Shaw used his historical knowledge, his analysis of social conditions, his native perception always to cut through from the particular example to the general trend or problem. It is his grasp of general conditions which gave his criticism so much acumen. He once set down the following general principles, worthy of quotation:

Now the theatre-going public may be divided roughly into three classes. First, a very small class of experts who know the exact value of the entertainment, and who do not give it a second trial if it does not please them. Second, a much larger class, which can be persuaded by puffs or by the general curiosity about a novelty which 'catches on', to accept it at twice or thrice its real value. Third, a mob of persons who, when their imaginations are excited, will accept everything at from ten times to a million times its real value, and who will, in this condition, make a hero of everybody who comes within their ken – manager, composer, author, comedian, and even critic. When a form of art, originally good enough to 'catch on', begins to go downhill as *opéra bouffe* did, the first class drops off at once; and the second, after some years, begins to follow suit gradually.

But the third class still worships its own illusion, and enjoys itself rather more than less as the stuff becomes more and more familiar, obvious, and vulgar . . .

Is that not a very shrewd observation about the various publics in a mass society? And is it not just what happened to 'the Proms' before their recent revival by William Glock?

Men like Shaw are rare in any case. Musical critics of his quality and verve are very rare. But it is not outside the bounds of imagination to believe that young critics of today, in their thirties, could train their sensibilities as Shaw did his, enabling them to make judgements of acumen and value. There are always general trends which need critical expression and clarification. There are always out-of-date modes and academic pedantries. There are always new voices struggling for a proper critical appreciation. Shaw believed that the critic must be tireless in his fight for standards and never satisfied. 'My own friends are those who give good performances', he once said. 'My enemies are those who in any way debase music.'

12 Persönliches Bekenntnis

This chapter has a German title, for the substance of it is a talk for the B.B.C. German Service; one of a series in which English personalities during the winter of 1957–8 spoke under the same title. 'Bekenntnis' is usually translated 'Confession', but rather in a sense of confession of faith than of sins. The talk had to be personal and, in a widely conceived sense, confessional.

There are many Englishmen who are so latin in their affiliations that the teuton in our blood is valueless to them; or vice versa. Others like myself know both. I find the exploration of these two foreign strands (for to be English is something different again) has meant a constant enrichment. When I divide and contrast them the latin is light and the teuton is dark. If I experienced them the other way round then it is clear A Child of Our Time *would have demanded a different imagery. If I bring the divisions together to marry them, there I seem to leave the known and divided Earth for some ideal Heaven. Walking the path are heroic figures who certainly lived and loved subject to Earth's rich impediments, yet knew the Heavens; like Dante and Goethe. Though I read Dante before Goethe I can truthfully say that neither now can invalidate the other.*

Broadcasting has a miraculous element by which one is in London yet one's voice issues in the homes of interested Germans. I have felt this more sharply still when I have broadcast to India; because behind the technical miracle by which the voice is carried, lie the enduring divisions which are not yet touched by this miracle at all. I consider this question more extensively in Chapter 14.

The kernel of my 'Personal Confession' is expressed in Jungian terms, because that is the language which seems the most precise for my purpose. If one is trusting that 'our desperate need and longing, as the tension of the opposites grows greater, will force a re-animation of the archetype of the God as Saviour'* one is, I think, believing that we shall have time. The suicidal lunacy of nuclear armament denies this *sense of time so sharply we cannot yet emotionally accept the naked fact of it. As I said in Chapter 2, that we go on creating and pro-creating, implies we have our sense of the future as yet intact. But the possibility of nuclear suicide is so recent we cannot yet esteem its challenge.*

I touched also in Chapter 2 on the possibility that the artist who has to animate his imaginative powers in order to create, thereby endangers partially or altogether at times his sense of reality. In my own experience this is a true possibility. One guards against it as a doctor guards against constant exposure to disease, or perhaps more exactly as a psychiatrist guards himself from the neuroses of his patients. I don't seem for myself to be able to escape it. The danger appears acutest during the preparation of those works which, as I discussed in Chapter 6, spring, to use Jungian jargon, from the Collective Unconscious. It is concerning such kinds of works that I quote in the following paper from Hölderlin and Goethe and Yeats.

Here I am in England. In England I live, and was born; half Celt, half Anglo-Saxon. In England are my bodily roots, and in England is my daily Present. If I think of Germany, where I have often been – or of France or of Italy – I feel indeed no barriers, but feel kinship, both racial and cultural. This racial kinship is of the past, not of the present. But I find that the cultural kinship with Europe, with all other lands indeed, tends also to recede into the past. I see English Alcuin at the Court of Charlemagne; I see the Irish monks at St Gall; or the sixteenth-century English lutanist, Dowland, home from Nuremberg from his travels in Germany and Italy. Just as a German might see Bach's youngest son in the London of Dr Johnson. For this sense of our cultural communion as chiefly in the past, is probably common to all of us. It is never like the sense of our daily Present, which is something quite other.

I am in England here and now – but in France or Germany too; because of the cultural kinship. This began perhaps when my Celtic ancestors had their homeland in bronze-age Bavaria, and becomes ever more defined and conscious as I imagine the years of history passing over from then till now. Or perhaps not quite till now. The first German I ever spoke was the German of Goethe. Of his time I think I am more conscious than of any other in Germany.

I am thinking too of Hölderlin. Not so much of the young Hölderlin of the nostalgically Greek *Hyperion*, but the Hölderlin of the late poems, when he became prophetic of the European madness into which we have since fallen. Sometimes Hölderlin feels that the older pre-Christian Gods are about to have a glorious reawakening. But more clearly he senses, that if indeed the many Gods of our pasts are coming to life again, it is not yet for our mental health.

The gay Gods of Greece were those he chiefly loved.

Aber Freund! Wir kommen zu spaet. Zwar leben die Goetter,
Aber ueber dem Haupt droben in anderer Welt.
Endlos wirken sie da und scheinen wenig zu achten,
Ob wir leben, so sehr schonen die Himmlischen uns,
Denn nicht immer vermag ein schwaches Gefaess sir zu fassen.

'But friend, we come too late. Truly the gods are alive, but up there in another world. They are endlessly active there and seem to mind little that we live, so well do they protect us, for a weak vessel cannot always contain them.'

But to be thus unable to sustain the Gods when they came, and to know them so only 'in another world', was deeply and prophetically bitter to him.

Zudessen duenket mir ofters besser zu schlafen, wie so ohne Genossen zu seyn,
So zu harren und was zu thun indess und zu sagen,
Weiss ich nicht, und wozu Dichter in duerftiger Zeit.

'Meantime I often think it better to sleep, being so without comrades, to have to wait so, and what to do and to say meanwhile I don't know, and what poets are for in a barren time.'

When I have pondered on the actuality of Hölderlin's 'und wozu Dichter in duerftiger Zeit' I am struck ever anew by the tremendous vitality and drive of the image-making faculty in man, which has since Hölderlin sustained, or rather forced, so many poets, painters, composers, to create in *immer duerftigerer Zeit*! – 'in an ever more barren time'. Naturally enough indeed I wonder at it, for I suffer this drive, within my limits, myself.

But let us think for the moment of Nietzsche, who certainly suffered both from the clear consciousness of the disintegration of our spiritual sensibility within an insatiable materialism, and from an inescapable creative drive; suffered, yet further, possession by a God. Jung, the Swiss psychologist, wrote just before the war a monograph suggesting that Nietzsche was possessed not in fact by Zarathustra, but by Wotan. If this is so, then perhaps it means that we can never dare to know consciously what God possesses us. I may, like Hölderlin, love the gay Greek Gods (though I must tremble before their dark and terrible natures), yet at the moment of intense creation, when music, if it is to live, must be searched for in those depths of the psyche where the god- and devil-images also hibernate; then how am I so sure, as I am, that I shall take no harm and the music be sane?

The answers are both personal and impersonal. Speaking impersonally first, I should answer that through Jung one can come to a viable, and partly even voluntary, relation with those psychic events, age-old predilections of the mind, which he calls the archetypes of the collective unconscious. Jung shows that there is as a psychological fact a *central* or centralizing predilection of the mind, an archetype of integration, of the union of opposites, of deity maybe, taking often the image of a human figure, the incarnation of a God or Saviour, of Christ or Buddha. This archetype he finds endlessly active in the human psyche, even in periods like the present, when the overt public values are entirely those of scientific materialism. So beyond mere hope, I believe there is now reasonable knowledge that our desperate need and longing, as the tension of the opposites grows greater, will force a re-animation of the archetype of the God as Saviour.

But Jung is quite clear that the longing for a more spiritually balanced life is still, for the vast mass of our people, pressed down into the unconscious by the dizzying social value given everywhere to the wonders of technics, and that this repressed longing, starved of the life-giving food of our attention and value, breeds violence and discontent. For we are still at the stage when to the individual alone, or shall we say, to certain individuals alone, comes at this time the inescapable duty to make conscious the repressed longing locked up in the inner violence and psychic disarray. But it follows, I am afraid, that any person driven along the path of integration, will by that in itself come into a polarity between his new values and the present overt values of our mass societies. Let him remember Hölderlin's 'weak vessel' and the price of Nietzsche's pride – and be humble.

Speaking now personally, I should answer that I cannot experience the archetype of integration in the direct way many others have done, because the creative artist is physically conditioned by the activities of the image-making drive which will not be gainsaid. My experience indeed is that most of the seemingly non-creative things an artist does – whether to take up teaching; to enter politics; to undertake Jungian analysis – are really phases of the inner creative life; and directed therefore to the ends of the art he practises. These non-creative activities are only secondary. I can never prosecute them for their own sake; even though for a time I feel sure I do, and only come to see the *real* and creative reason later on. Although therefore I may never know the fullness of personal integration, so that I may give an example in my daily life of one willing and able to sustain the polarity between his new private values and the public old, I can yet know that the sympathies of my art lie with these possibilities; and more important still, know that my art might form a tiny fragment of the great mirror, in which we see our unconscious longings reflected as images that have power to change us whither we must go. Goethe wrote somewhere:

> Und umzuschaffen das Geschaffene
> Dass sich's nicht zum Starren waffne
> Wirkt ewiges lebendiges Thun.†

Think what an extraordinary piece of the mirror this process led to in *Faust 2*! Is not the creator almost already mad to search for poetry in such depths? But is not the work of art inexhaustible and, if strange, magically sanc? As Yeats put the matter differently, in a letter: 'I can entirely understand the excitement a God feels on getting into a statue.'

†Translation on p. 103

*It is clear from the Postscript to Part 2 that in 1974 I find the expression 'God as Saviour' to delineate this archetype much too ambivalent.

13 The Artist's Mandate

Hölderlin is a moving example of the Socratic madness which I speak of in this chapter. For he enjoyed the divine madness of poetic creation, yet suffered long periods of alienation into a clinical madness. If I am right in suggesting, in the previous chapter, that the artist's job as such carries with it the constant, though for most of us mild, danger of impairing the sense of reality, then Hölderlin's real madness was in some way connected with his divine madness. But how, we do not know.

Is the word 'madness' the key-word which induces us to think that Freud or Jung can help us understand better how artistic imagination functions? Jung seems to suggest that the artist with certain sensibilities is driven to explore deep levels of collective unconsciousness in order to bring forth images which by their fascination and power will compel us against every intellectual objection to re-order our lives. I state it in this deliberately crude way so that Jung's therapeutic preoccupations are clear. There is great danger in Freud's or Jung's theories of art of losing sight of the aesthetic in its own right. Greek tragedy is a perhaps too happy hunting-ground for depth psychology. One cannot see however what either Freud or Jung contributes to understanding the emotion we feel before old Chinese vases.

Again, stated in the way I did, Jung's theory seems to throw the accent all upon the future. Yet part of the aesthetic emotion is an immediacy of appreciation, of the ineffable moment exactly present now. We can be struck by the beauty of a Wren church in the middle of ugly London, by something momentarily there, yet eternal, neither past nor future. Or by Mozart reaching us on disc or radio through an opened window. I am unsure whether modern art does this for us in the same degree. 'Here the men of today and the men of yesterday must part company. Anyone whose ears do not burn, whose eyes do not cloud over at the thought of the concentration camps, the crematoriums, the atomic explosions which make up our reality – at the *dissonances of the music, the broken tattered forms of our painting, the lament of Dr Faustus – is free to crawl into the shelter of the safe old methods and rot.' With sensibilities tuned to such a temper, what sort of art shall we get? 'We must acknowledge the evil, the blackness, the disintegration which cry to us so desperately from the art of our time, and whose presence it so desperately affirms.'* The ineffable moments will be harder won.*

This paper was prepared as a radio talk, but, for reasons I have forgotten, never spoken.

That the artist, whether composer, poet or painter, has a special gift, no one ever denies. But how valuable we think this gift is to society and what is its real function there; these are matters not of fact but of opinion. A chess-playing genius has a special gift; or to take an example of more bodily endowment, a world-record-breaking athlete has a gift. Are these special faculties of the same kind as the image-making faculty of the artist? And again, even if we take them to be somehow of the same kind, do we hold them of the same value?

I have no idea how old in history is the chess-playing gift, but it is difficult to see how it existed before the invention of chess; so here is a truly remarkable, and quite unpredictable, gift which appears out of the blue, but directed specifically to the game of chess – to a limited social accomplishment, useless of course in a society which has never heard of chess. I suppose that in these non-chess-playing societies other specifically directed social gifts appear. Whatever they are they will hardly be more mysterious than the birth of a chess genius.

Now while we agree that a gift for chess playing cannot be older than societies which play chess, and have played chess presumably for centuries, we might suppose that transcendent athletics, that is the combination of a fine physique with a certain mental temperament, had always existed. But it is not quite so simple as that. There are many old societies of folk of remarkable physique, especially in Africa, which would appear to have had no social interest in athletics as we understand it. We call the world festival of athletics an Olympic Games, and that is the only true name, because athletics, in this sense, is of Greek origin

*. Erich Neumann, 'Art & Time'; from *Man & Time* (Routledge & Kegan Paul).

dating from the four-yearly festivals at Olympia. These festivals were intensely social, and indeed, at least initially, religious. The games were held in honour of Olympian Zeus and began and ended with ritual. During the period of the games all wars in Greece temporarily stopped. Is part of our present tremendous social interest in athletics and the Olympic Games because we respond to anything which begins with individual virtue yet lifts us right out of our single selves to some other plane? The Greeks made statues of their Olympic winners and set them up in the precincts of Zeus's temple. In a sense we are doing the same.

So I am quite clear that athletics, even if we have lost the Greek tradition of human beauty which was mixed with it, is a very intense social interest indeed – potentially an ennobling one – perhaps even an aesthetic one. Or rather, to keep to matters of fact, athletics in its origin was not only well-being and bodily discipline, but a part of worship, and worthy of music, poetry and sculpture.

There were older societies which did not develop this amalgam of fine physique and bodily beauty to honour the gods; but it is clear that the gift of creating images, the special gift of the artist, is as old as man himself. The prehistoric cave paintings which go back before the last ice-age are astonishing, not just because our prehistoric ancestors drew recognizable bison in the dark depths of their caves, but because in face of these drawings and paintings we have the same fundamental artistic emotions as before any art of historical times. Not that we can ever explain or define what these artistic emotions are; the point is that we know them when we feel them (even if they may be felt in a very simple and primitive way, in the pleasure of just *looking* at a streamlined car) and we feel them in an extremely powerful form before the art of the cave-men.

To return to the Greeks: they discussed eagerly the nature of these aesthetic emotions. They hoped to tabulate and rationalize them, but they admitted too that there were irrational elements in the process of artistic creation which could not be explained. As the Greeks said of themselves it depended whether you were under the influence of the God Apollo, or the God Dionysus. In a dialogue of Plato, Phaedrus asks Socrates, as they lay in the shade talking by the little stream of Ilyssus, how he thinks artists gain a true sense of their art. And Socrates answers:

'If you mean how can one become a finished artist, then probably – indeed I may say undoubtedly – it is the same as with anything else: if you have an innate gift for art, you will become a famous artist, provided you also acquire knowledge and practise; but if you lack any of these three you will be correspondingly unfinished.'

Is not that a splendidly up-to-date and lucid answer? It is Socrates speaking under the influence of Apollo. But it might also be any modern rationalizing psychologist. We sort out the basic elements and name them as: innate gift, knowledge, and practice. In so far as we understand what they are, gift, knowledge and practice are basic. They remain unchanging characteristics and necessities of artistic production for all time.

Yet Socrates was well aware that innate gift is a question-begging term. Looked at from another point of view it begs the very question we want to ask: What is the nature of the 'innate gift' upon which *art* builds, by knowledge and practice? And Socrates gives a very famous, but also much debated answer.

He considers first whether what we call madness might not really be of two kinds. One kind is clearly a disease – the rational mind being disordered and unamenable to the will – and even if we picture it as though the sufferer's personality has been possessed by some other and alien personality, yet this possession is unhealthy and often markedly anti-social. But the other kind might be a madness, where the invading personality, though unaccountable and irrational, is yet beneficent and creative; possession not by a devil, but by a god.

Socrates thinks there are four common examples of divine madness. The first is that of the prophet, such as the oracle at Delphi. The second is the madness or frenzy which expiates inherited guilt. (This is peculiarly Greek, and hardly touches us in those terms – though Mr Eliot's *The Family Reunion* is a modern play about it.) The fourth is the madness of the lover – especially divine when the passion of love leads to love of beauty and wisdom through the beauty and wisdom of the beloved person. And creative art is the third. As Socrates tells Phaedrus: 'There is a third form of possession or madness, of which the Muses are the source. This seizes a tender, virgin soul and stimulates it to rapt passionate expression, especially in lyric poetry . . . But if any man come to the gates of poetry without the madness of the Muses, persuaded that skill alone will make him a good poet, then shall he and his works of sanity with him be brought to naught by the poetry of madness and see their place is nowhere to be found.'

I find that a splendid admission of the irrational, unaccountable elements in creative art. It is Socrates speaking under the influence of Dionysus. But it is also strangely similar to the findings and views of modern depth psychology. Re-fashion the language a bit and it would be up to date.

But even if we can make Plato sound up to date, we cannot do away with all the twenty-three centuries in between as though they had not happened. Plato's account of artistic inspiration did in fact remain more or less unchallenged – and we all recognize it in a well-worn passage of Shakespeare. But after Shakespeare in the following century, the dynamic and direction of social interest underwent a change. Art and interest in art continued, but a new element began increasingly to gather to itself the energy of social interest – that element was science. It is such a well-known story that I need not repeat it here. All we have to consider now is what this increasing social interest in science and technics, this fascination which scientific technics exercised, what it did to the social idea of art, not to the process of art itself. And it did a great deal. For as the social interest went over increasingly to technics, to all those reasonable and predictable things which science discovers for us, so the society at large lost interest, and in the end lost understanding of that irrational and unpredictable element in the works of artists, without which, as Socrates put it 'their place is nowhere to be found'.

I may make this clear by considering some personalities of our own century; and first Einstein. Einstein, by a process extraordinarily like artistic creation, produced theories about the universe we live in, which turned topsy-turvy the scientific picture established in the main by Leibnitz and Newton, in the century after Shakespeare. And Einstein's picture of the universe is furthermore so strange and difficult few of the rest of us know what it is at all. Even the scientists disagree. If men go in rockets to stars at incredible speeds will they grow as old as if they had stayed on earth? Or to put it in more neutral terms – will the clocks on board the rocket really go slower, or only appear to? Perhaps the trouble starts with what we mean by the word 'appear'. But my immediate point here is that Einstein's world picture is very difficult if not impossible for laymen to understand; yet no one has any doubt of his greatness and of his social value. We are more ready to put up a statue of him in the precincts of Zeus's temple, than of Gordon Pirie or Zatopek.

But now let me turn to a figure on the borders of science, to Freud, the inventor of psychoanalysis. Here was someone who also turned our picture of things, or rather our picture of ourselves, topsy-turvy. And the results, for which Freud certainly claimed scientific justification, have been perhaps more devastating. But it is clear we are much less ready to consider him great, in the way we conceded greatness to Einstein. For with Freud, however scientific he felt himself to be, we come close to irrational and incalculable forces; indeed to the most irrational and powerful of them all; the emotion, drive, instinct we call sex. However much sex is neutralized, tabulated, rationalized – de-sexed in fact – in order to bring it within the boundaries of our divine science, yet in *ourselves*, in persons and living societies, it is an incalculable power that stems from a very different god than the god of science. As the Greeks put it, even all-powerful Zeus succumbed at times to the power of the gods of sex, Eros and Aphrodite.

Freud speaks with the voice of millions because he speaks of our inner drives. But we do not like it; we may even be afraid. And fear, especially unconscious fear, turns easily to anger and to hate. To use Freud's language, we project upon him, or his ideas, our fury at being made aware of the inevitable violence and irrationality of the sexual forces within the body of our private life. The unwished awareness was all the more resented because it came to a society not open like that of the Greeks, but self-restricting, as was European society in the Victorian age of Freud's youth.

And now let me name two of the giants in creative art of our time: Stravinsky and Picasso. What social value does mass society accord to them? The answer is inescapable: none. They, or rather their works, live only on the fringe of the mass society proper. Their names and their reputations may be perhaps widely known, but not their works.

Now just as sex, though hopelessly refractory to our scientific attitude, cannot be suppressed or charmed away, so it is true of the desire for art. But if real social value is not in fact given to art, because given to science, then the sensibilities and faculties we employ when we give rein to our desires for art are not those with which we design and make our precision instruments, but our more primitive and untrained ones – occasionally, even some of our debased ones. And from this amalgam of instinctive desire for art with untrained and unformed sensibilities arises that phenomenon which we are all familiar with – mass based entertainment. All the mass based entertainment in the world cannot add up to a half-pennyworth of great art.

What happens then to the creators of great art, if such there be, in a time when the real social value is given to science and mass entertainment?

To return first to the point about reputation and works. A friend of mine, a Swiss conductor, who with his wife has long been a generous patron of individual artists, put the matter to me rather well, when we were talking this summer. He said: 'An artist at the present moment is never really being paid for his creative work, but only for his publicity value.' He did not mean this cynically. He was just stating a fact – and in his opinion a welcome fact. The creative artist can and does put up a semblance of living within the values of the mass society of our day. He can do this and thereby get a livelihood with greater or less success, it seems, in either Communist or Capitalist society; that is in such industrialized societies as exist. But this only makes all the more mysterious what he is doing in relation to society when he creates. So back we are where we began.

I suggested before that Socrates' description of the irrational and incalculable element in creative art was close to the findings of modern depth psychology. I was thinking of Jung rather than Freud. Jung has made an exhaustive study of the image-making faculty of the psyche, not because he has great aesthetic interest in modern art, but because he finds that part of this faculty, especially when the images come free, in dreams, and visions, is supremely beneficial to us, if we are in psychological trouble. These spontaneous images which arise from within present often a complementary or even opposed view of things to that of our rational, or conventional conscious mind; and during the process of living with and studying these images as they appear, the inner attitude changes, in such a way that it becomes more attuned to reality than before. Naturally enough this therapeutic view of spontaneous dreams and visions has led Jung rather to the study of religious psychology than of art. But he shows too how the artist *also* speaks with the voice of millions when the images he plays with come from the depths of the collective psyche. And yet this voice of millions may be only a voice to come; because the collective images may as yet be only complementary, or downright opposed to the prevailing conscious values of the time. The new images that break first upon the world through this or that great artist, will only slowly be accepted, as the general attitude changes in their direction. And though the public may entirely reject the new images at their appearance, the art will nevertheless stay, because of the power it has from expressing the sensibilities which will appear. It is not easy to make all this crystal clear, without difficulties and even mystifications. But that description is at least of something dynamic not static. And the confusions and mystifications come chiefly from the extreme difficulty of dealing in static terms with a dynamic process.

Of course, confusion is not confined to artistic matters. Economics would provide another example; especially the economics of any dynamic society, or the economics of the accumulation of capital in the present in order to have much more of something in years to come. Now a creative artist is doing exactly that. He is accumulating our artistic capital, the results of which will last for long after his own death. And to accumulate this kind of capital is his unwritten mandate. There is no question in our day of the artist receiving a true mandate from *society* to create. The mandate of society is to entertain, and that mandate is clear and uncomplicated. But the mandate of the artist's own nature, of his special and innate gift, is to reach down into the depths of the human psyche and bring forth the tremendous images of things to come. These images are not yet art. It takes a lifetime's work to mould them into works of art. For this the artist can have no reward but in the joy of doing it. He creates, because without art, in this deep and serious sense, the nation dies. His mandate is inescapable.

14 Too Many Choices

I said in Chapter 10 that the attempt 'to come at the feel of our time led to Chapter 14', which is to the following essay. I did not mean that strictly only the desire to contrast the feel of Mozart's time with our own led to this chapter, for it is plain enough that I was circling round this problem already in Chapter 1. The precise beginning for the essay, the moment when my mind became aware of a seemingly new way in, was a half-sentence by the painter Kokoschka. Kokoschka wrote a kind of manifesto at the end of the last war, which he entitled: A Petition from a Foreign Artist to the Righteous People of Gt Britain for a Secure and Present Peace. It is a considerable petition and quite early on appears the half-sentence, printed in bold type: '... A FALLACY IS BLURRING THE CLEAR DISTINCTION BETWEEN WHAT IS IN AND WHAT IS OUT OF THE MIND.' I am puzzled by the word 'fallacy', but on inquiry Kokoschka sent me a message that it is what he meant; there is no question of mistranslation, for he wrote his Petition in English. If we discard the word 'fallacy' and think again of those names in the last chapter, Einstein and Freud, we can sense that whether we turn our eye into space or into the psyche, we are confronted with ambiguity and relativity. Surely this is part of what is 'blurring the clear distinction between what is in and what is out of the mind'?

Or to take an example from politics: the Iron Curtain is both an external fact of electrically wired fences and minefields and an internal attitude. The attitude engenders the dividing frontier and the Curtain, the Curtain then reinforces the attitude. The impasse becomes exceedingly difficult and dangerous to remove, and induces violence of all kinds. How can we avoid this inevitable violence unless we have first disentangled the attitude from the gestures? I doubt if we have the means at all yet to distinguish between an external fact like human pigmentation and the inner attitude of a colour bar. Or to locate exactly that part of oneself which is Christian, if one confesses that faith, in converse with a Moslem or a Hindu, seeing that the Moslem or the Hindu is equally confused by the 'blurring of the clear distinction between what is in and what is out of the mind'.

Yet this fascinating aphorism of Kokoschka does not appear in the essay following, because I found it too stimulating, too exhaustive. It belongs to the same class of ideas as the Confucian Rectification of the Names. Neither Kokoschka nor I are true philosophers, so we are not equipped or gifted to rectify the names, or to unblur the clear distinctions between what is in and what is out of the mind in all the endless ways the blurring operates in modern life. I imagine indeed the blurring is a perennial problem in times of confusion and transition; as indeed China has known already more than one period when the Confucian Rectifications were appropriate. But Einstein and Freud, in the sense I spoke of them in the last chapter, have accentuated our feeling of relativity, and perhaps thereby of insecurity, in a way which seems new to us as we suffer it.

I tried to limit the scope and range of themes, and achieved only partial success. I began with the ideas of East and West, only of course to find that these are as blurred as anything else of their kind. They are geographical entities, yet also historical political attitudes. (What in the ideas is outside the mind and what in?) But they served as an entry, because it is possible to ask ourselves questions with these blurred counters which can help us towards the feel of our own time by comparison with an earlier time. Thus I ask what East and West meant to Columbus and mean to us. I then contrast the view of our one world as seen from an artificial satellite in orbit, which might be called the view outside the mind, with the view a Hindu can have of a Moslem, or a Christian of a Moslem, which might be called part of the view inside the mind.

Inevitably I have eventually to reduce the 'we' of my discourse from Mankind in general, through the endless divisions to the class of men of which I have a specialist knowledge; to creative artists. I then consider how much they need to be aware of the manifest complexities of our time. How they fare if they are convinced Christians, or if they are agnostic. How they sustain themselves without and within against the tremendous social interest in technology. How they are to act if the technologically interested society in which they may be caught by the blurring fact of an Iron Curtain or a Colour Bar, is absolutely inimical to any spontaneity that has power. In all this I speak of the creative artist in his prime and maturity. I am not really considering *Jimmy Porter*.

Then there is the problem of Time. This seems to me so strange that I do not discuss it properly in the paper at all. I merely evasively state it. If there is only one meaning of Time – historical time in a straight line – then it is an anguished matter if one's society is like Poland continuously and absolutely in the Path of History, as we have known it so far, or like England where our Island fortress has for centuries not suffered the armies of the invader. Can Poland never be free? The Polish intellectual often despairs, as he does now. But I can imagine the Polish peasant may survive with his dumb vitality unimpaired because his sense of Time is not of this historical kind, but of an eternal renewal in which every spring is the miraculously pristine sprouting of the new corn. If through our deepening sense of relativity and insecurity within, and our nuclear armaments without, we all, English and Polish alike, stand equally in the Path of History, what then? Shall we like the peasant find Time as a straight line inadequate, because too frightening, and will the other sense of Time, of an eternal return, sustain us better? Or are these two senses of Time really complementary and in some unexplained way both necessary, even though superficially and intellectually they seem contradictory? Buried within this problem, at any rate for me, is the further sense of moments which are out of Time altogether.

Lastly by a rather abrupt transition I move from the two senses of Time to the two ways of art: abstraction and humanism. I do not suggest these dualities are analogies, for we do not experience them as such. But I think the deep relationship between all dualities is a problem of abiding fascination for me. I return to it again and again. I find it reflected in such seemingly contradictory figures as D. H. Lawrence and Blake. I may not experience the division and the copulation in Laurentian or Blakeian terms – I am neither a novelist nor a mystic; but I cannot escape the special impact of any art which seems to be the product of a marriage. Lines of a Rilke sonnet haunt my mind:

> Nur wer die Leier schon hob
> auch unter Schatten
> darf das unendliche Lob
> ahnend erstatten.*

*. 'Only he who raised his lyre also under shadows, may with divining tongue sound the infinite praise.'

Recently I have been thinking again about two Renaissance figures: Columbus and Galileo. The Columbus who first occupied my attention was the *Christophe Colombe* of Claudel, through the stimulus of the recent visit of the Jean-Louis Barrault Company. But, of course, Claudel's way of responding to the Columbus story soon gave place in my mind to a response more consistent with my own interests and predilections – which may be only a way of saying with my prejudices.

Like Claudel, I nearly always find it impossible to remain for long responding to a past historical period without my present interests bit by bit demanding attention, until they soon occupy once more the whole mental field. So the past, which has stimulated the train of thought, becomes only a means to illumine the present. Not of course as pure history, because I am emphatically no historian; nor as politics or economics; nor as anthropology or archaeology, and so on: but as sensibility.

Columbus sailed off to the West to reach the East. But, as we all know, he never found the East by going West. He found a continent in between – a new West; the New World. From my present point of view it is the fact of this New World, and not the fact that the earth was soon proved to be round, not flat, which matters; because though the first ship to sail right round the world and back into port was an image which forced men to see the earth in an absolutely new form, the very fact of a New World to the West, where men might begin again in communities free from tyranny and prejudice and tradition, gave reality to dreams and impulses, which deepened into a whole continent of new experience. And we can now take up in mental hands and finger this American amalgam of flight from tyranny and tradition, dream of communal innocence and good, stimulus of adventure and hard struggle to push a frontier ever back to the West and finally into the sea. After that there is no more frontier.

Very well then, there is no more frontier; but is that a final fact? In Russia now, is the adventure and hard struggle to push the frontier back to the east, over the Siberian tundra, part of the same human experience as the wild American West? I do not think so. For there is no place in the Russian amalgam, that I know of, for flights from political tyranny and traditionalism, or dreams of simple innocence and good. The centre of the experience seems to be the overwhelming social stimulus of the industrialization of a peasant people, flowing to the eastern seaboard in a vast wave of economic expansion following upon the planned and deliberate surveys. Against this overwhelming social experience, the horrors of the Siberian labour camps, where those at odds with Soviet society are certainly not free as folk were free on the American frontier – against this overwhelming social experience, the horrors seem . . . ? That is a question which must come up again later.

In England now the overriding dynamic of mechanization (the new factories, new industrial techniques) is not so socially universal, although, in my opinion, just as fundamental. We compartmentalize our social life more easily. We can, as academics for example, or as artists, inhabit smaller worlds where the social primacy of technological advance can appear as a monstrous philistinism. But that too is a matter which must come later.

Englishmen who are directly responsive to the stimulus of technocracy, on the other hand, and who may be exported to the dark continent of Africa, find no true frontier there, but, like their Russian colleagues in Siberia, find the inexhaustible appetite for industrialization. Oil, diamonds, hydro-electric power, uranium – these seem to be the value-words, and engineer the honorific title.

This will hardly seem strange in so primitive a country as Africa. It can be made to seem strange, at any rate more complicated, in lands with centuries of civilization to their history, like India or China. Yet there it is for all to see. And there the circle completes itself. The industries of China flow north to meet the industries of Siberia, or east to face Japan. Japan looks across the Pacific to the one-time American frontier. That is exactly the view that sputnik has, encircling the globe so many times in the day. Sputnik tells us that now at last the world is round. With its mechanized voice it is an image of a scarcely credible scientific age. It is the frothy bauble of the unappeasable urge to industrialize the world. It is on its dark side the herald of ever more limitless weapons of warfare, youngest brain-children of our unappeasable death-wish.

Sputnik, then, with the superficial vision of its technological eye, saw that the world is one. But emotionally one – that we certainly are not. For instance, sputniks go far too fast to observe locality. But for all the free or forced migrations of our time, 99 per cent of mankind still live in a locality. And localities have cultural traditions so old, they flow in the blood-stream. Consider the ending of that rich, unforgettable attempt to stretch the sensibility to cover East and West – I mean the novel *A Passage to India*; the last meeting of the Indian and the Englishman, the falling back from friendship, each man marrying back into his own race :

Fielding mocked again. And Aziz in an awful rage danced this way and that, not knowing what to do, and cried: 'Down with the English, anyhow. That's certain. Clear out, you fellows, double quick, I say. We may hate one another, but we hate you most. If I don't make you go, Ahmed will, Karim will, if it's fifty-five-hundred years we shall get rid of you; yes, we shall drive every blasted Englishman into the sea, and then' – he rode against him furiously – 'and then,' he concluded, half kissing him, 'you and I shall be friends.'

'Why can't we be friends now?' said the other, holding him affectionately. 'It's what I want. It's what you want.'

But the horses didn't want it – they swerved apart; the earth didn't want it, sending up rocks through which the riders must pass single file; the temples, the tank, the jail, the palace, the birds, the carrion, the Guest House, that came into view as they issued from the gap and saw Mau beneath: they didn't want it, they said in their hundred voices, 'No, not yet,' and the sky said, 'No, not there.'

But change the horses to motors, and change the characters appropriately; deaden the sensibility and repress religious feeling; then newer and other voices will say, 'Yes, yes, now,' and the aeroplanes in the sky will say, 'Yes, yes, here'.

Yet we cannot all deaden the sensibility or repress religious feeling. And what happens to us then in our one world ? I want to quote now from an essay by T. S. Eliot called *What is a Classic?* For in this essay Eliot considers this question within the strictest limits of locality, as referring exclusively to Europe, to Rome, to Virgil. Yet all is discussed as applicable to ourselves now. And it is in this sense one must appreciate this half-sentence: 'The Roman Empire and the Latin language were not any Empire and any language, but an Empire and a language with a unique destiny in relation to ourselves.'

If we look at this statement carefully, we soon see that it is only provocative at its end. That is to say, we understand the words 'the Roman Empire and the Latin language' in a reasonably conventional and agreed sense, even though we know now that the Roman Empire seems quite different in the history books of Arabs or Turks. (Is not the European heritage of the Empire and the language being rejected now in Algeria?) But with the words 'a unique destiny in relation to ourselves' we can be provoked into a sharper awareness of their import.

The sense of a 'unique destiny' allies itself in my mind with the notion of Christianity's beginning at a single and unique moment in time, and with the peculiar sense of history, even perhaps Marxian history, that this Christian sensibility engenders. But certainly the Hindu has no such sense of a unique destiny. Nor has the Buddhist. So we are forced back on the strict limitations to the last word in Eliot's half-sentence, the word 'ourselves'. And this 'ourselves' is the same as in an earlier Eliot essay, where he is discussing the spiritual vacuum caused by lack of a religion, and in which he says: '... And for us religion means the Christian religion.'

Clearly, then, Mr Eliot's 'us' is not always Mr Forster's 'us', even though their blood is the same. And we cannot escape the question as to whether Mr Forster's imaginative experience, which forced him to stretch his sensibility from us to them, over the divisions of the blood, is to be more commended in our one world, just for this reason, than that part of Mr Eliot's imaginative experience which forces him to accept all the limits of the locality and to glory in its unique tradition. Like the climax of Auden's 'Hymn to St Cecilia': 'O wear your tribulation like a rose.'

For there is a splendid arrogance, perhaps even prophetic arrogance, in a later sentence of Eliot's essay on *What is a Classic?* which begins: 'We need to remind ourselves that ... Europe is ... still, in its progressive mutilation and disfigurement, the organism out of which any great world harmony must develop...'

'Europe is still...' That is the rose. But further on again, I get an inkling of the tribulation. There is a sentence which runs: 'So we may think of Roman literature: at first sight a literature of limited scope, with a poor muster of great names, yet universal as no other literature can be; a literature unconsciously sacrificing, in compliance to its destiny in Europe, the opulence and variety of later tongues, to produce, for us, the classic.'

'Unconsciously sacrificing' ... 'for us'; that is the tribulation. And behind this 'unconscious sacrifice', in the literary and cultural sense, lies another sacrifice; that which has half-turned any poet anywhere, every creative artist, into an outsider. But to discuss this I must return to Galileo.

My original stimulus to think about Galileo came from Brecht's last play: *Leben des Galilei*, which I have read but not seen. Brecht's own stimulus to write the play was the news of the splitting of the atom. He uses the life of Galileo to dramatize the political and social problems of modern science. He shows us Galileo, after the torture by the Inquisition, publicly confessing to untruth, in the confident knowledge that truth once published must prevail, because truth is independent of all conscientious questions, such as his own personal behaviour before the Inquisition. Brecht's Galileo, as he no doubt intended, is an equivocal hero. And to us who read the play now, knowing that Brecht wrote it before the war, there is an added irony, because Galileo's personal behaviour (the private lie as public confession) is so humanly similar to the sorry spectacle of the many degrading confessions under totalitarian Communism, as Brecht might himself have experienced bodily, had his exile from Nazi Germany been in Russia and not in the United States.

Yet Galileo's science, as Brecht clearly saw, had an objective truth that was indeed to prevail if – and that is the important proviso – it was upheld by social pressure. I do not mean 'social' in only a narrow, Marxist sense. I mean social also in the sense of an emotional dynamic which rises from generation to generation from the collective psyche, until one social constellation, say in this case medieval Christianity, with its symbols of Heaven and Hell, Trinity and Virgin, goes slowly over into an opposed constellation, say then into rationalistic Enlightenment, with its God of Science and Devil of Superstition, its Atom and Ray and Quantum.

It seems to me a desperate waste of energy not to face the fact that changes of social constellation in this sense effect temporarily quite absolute changes of social status. Yet while within the community as a whole the status thus changes, the person is, just as before, born with an undeniable and individual gift and faculty. If under one constellation of society men with scientific interests and faculties are socially negligible until with the rising tide they become dangerous – and Giordano Bruno is sent from the Inquisition to the stake: then under another constellation of society men with religious and poetic faculties, desirable to themselves personally, become absolutely negligible socially. Under the strain they have committed suicide – many have gone mad.

I have, of course, deliberately over-simplified the argument so that I could dramatize it – just as I dramatized the problems of local tradition within a technologically round world in the persons of Mr Eliot and Mr Forster – and just as I began to dramatize the political problems of an overwhelming social need to industrialize one's backward country by reference to the Soviet labour camps in Siberia.

I think everyone chooses and everyone sacrifices. In the first instance the choices and sacrifices are involuntary. We are born into such-and-such a society, which has a particular set of dominant values to which it gives absolute status. And we are born with such-and-such gifts and faculties. Most people's faculties allow them to grow up in sympathy with the rising or reigning social dynamic. If that be named their choice, then their sacrifice is simply of those values which the reigning social dynamic suppresses. The sacrifice, like the choice, is unconscious. They only become aware of the matter through contact with those whose gifts do not permit them to grow up in sympathy with the conventional scale of values. Or they begin themselves to be temporarily unbalanced by the force of the repressed values rising unbidden from within.

If they examined these repressed values seriously, then of course they would at once realize their dangerous contradiction to the conventional modes of the time. Therefore the usual course is to consult a psychiatrist as to methods of restoring the sense of social fitness. And where the psychiatrist is able to do this, then he receives as much social status as the doctor.

But for the negligible minority, born like everyone else into the society of their time but whose individual fate it is, through the accident of their special gift or the persistence of their psychic unbalance, to become increasingly aware of those values which their time has refused and of the repressed violence within the society that has sacrificed too much – for this negligible minority the problems of which choice and what sacrifice, or which stimulus and what response, are intricate and complex. For in our one world of no more frontiers there are too many choices offered for any one person to accept them all. And so the person who becomes aware of the matter has ever to take stock of his position to see how he is to behave satisfactorily in society at all.

To repeat: even if a majority do make easily and naturally the socially adapted response within their community, they are in fact the prisoners of the choice (between one social constellation and another) which the community as a whole has made, or is making. But to be thus prisoners within a dominant social attitude is to make a sacrifice inside the individual psyche; the sacrifice of those sensibilities and apprehensions which have virtually no social status – none, at least, when pitted against the terrific overwhelming power of the socially conventional. And further, that just so fast as a man is made aware of this personal sacrifice, whether by natural temperament or by the complementary power of psychic disturbance, just so fast is he moving away from the prisoner's base of the socially adapted, towards the no-man's-land of the socially questionable. If the psychiatrist leads him safely back to prisoners' base, then all is well. If he does not get back to prisoners' base, he becomes a member of the negligible minority at odds with their society. And that is a different matter.

It is another matter again, though allied, when we are born with interests and faculties which can be socially fulfilled only in opposition to the dominant attitude. As Yeats put it, in his incomparable and personal imagery:

> Conduct and work grow coarse, and coarse the soul,
> What matter? Those that Rocky Face holds dear,
> Lovers of horses and of women, shall,
> From marble of a broken sepulchre,
> Or dark betwixt the polecat and the owl,
> Or any rich, dark nothing disinter
> The workman, noble and saint, and all things run
> On that unfashionable gyre again.

To many members of Yeats's profession this sort of thing has seemed like whistling in the dark to keep the courage up. I would myself say that if fine poetry is to be made out of the artist's present predicament, then Yeats is a master in this manner. (It is more difficult, I think, to discern how this general problem affects music and painting.) And if fine poetry is read and enjoyed, then the predicament of the negligible minority seems by that to have meaning also for the majority. But that would probably be a rash conclusion. It argues, I think, in too logical a manner.

By calling on Yeats to speak, I have narrowed the negligible minority down to that handful of men and women whose fate it is to be gifted with spontaneous artistic vision. Yet at the risk of repetition I must make it clear I know, too, that the experimental scientist is also burdened with a creative gift. The point I am stressing is that in a scientific age like ours the scientist feels his gift to have 100 per cent social value, while the artist knows that his gift, according to his nation, has $\frac{1}{2}$ to 2 per cent value. (These figures are dramatic, not scientific!)

Viewed from sputnik, our world is round and much the same all over. Sputnik has a superbly technological soul. I am sure his proper pride is really in this technology, and not in the political accident that the first of his race was Russian. The round world of science, whether communist or capitalist, is confident. It will go on inventing everything, however risky, because it is upheld by unimpeachable status. The social pressure which sustains this status is still incomparably more powerful than that which gives us qualms in the stomach about total destruction.

This being so it would seem that the predicament of the creative artist in relation to such society is the same the world over. From the lofty view of sputnik this is so; but on the ground of the locality it is less so. In a community like modern Russia or modern China, where the drive to industrialize a backward country has so overwhelming a social pressure behind it, many humane values can, indeed perhaps must, be neglected. I am sure all Russian women in cities want, with part of their femininity, to dress like the women of Paris. But with another part of themselves they submit willingly to the absolute social priorities which the drive to industrialization demands. In the same way I doubt if the Russians, as a nation, are so very much more harsh than the rest of us; so if and when they are able to turn their social eyes from the five-year plans, they may abolish the labour camps altogether.

As for the creative artist, to return to him again, he may be also, by his very function perhaps, a humane value which can, indeed perhaps must, be neglected. We all know that the artist entertainer in Russia, as in the West, has tremendous position. He is like the psychiatrist who guides the temporarily astray back to prisoners' base. So too the creative artist, who can give expression to the necessity of industrialization: he is like the pep-talk purveyor, the comrade in the party pulpit. But the creative artist whose fate it is to be like the analytical psychologist in face of spontaneously generated individuation – he is lost. He is silent and dead.

People like myself, the permitted if negligible minority of the West, can never be properly balanced in this matter, unless we keep trust and feel sympathy with the men and women who are born into such totally driven societies – born with God-given apprehensions and faculties that are technologically unwanted. What happens to them I do not know. Within the triumphs of their community theirs is a personally tragic destiny. God, or nature, has chosen them in the first place, and they grow up to fulfil that choice. Then there comes the socially inevitable sacrifice. They are indeed 'as though they had never been born'.

I must admit that I can never get these silent colleagues quite out of my mind. I find them to be, for me at any rate, a kind of absolute. They are born with a gift to respond to a certain challenge and they try to make that response. Their society lives under pressure from a different challenge and demands certain other responses. This predicament then becomes, to the man who suffers it, a kind of challenge – and I dread to think what kind of personal response it sometimes demands.

But such sympathy as one may feel also sets a problem. For it seems to me unrealistic not to make with one side of ourselves a generous response to the grand historical spectacle of huge nations dragging themselves up industrially by their boot-strings. Yet if one's choice is to live by certain neglected humane values, one may have to sacrifice that kind of response, because one needs to be true to one's nature, whether East or West. If one chooses and sacrifices in this way, then one does; without invalidating by that choice or that sacrifice (even the tragic sacrifice of one's death) the accepted values of one's society. The more open we become to stimulus, the more drastic, personally, may have to be the response; because the stimulus is contradictory and complex. There is no more frontier.

Returning to an earlier matter, we know that however stubborn the local traditions remain, the varieties of culture from all over the round world impinge on us more and more. So there is a kind of choice to be made here too – as between one tradition and another; or as between local and global? I do not want to repeat what has been mentioned above through the voices of Mr Eliot and Mr Forster. I should like to add only that maybe the important challenge is to awareness. Even if a writer writes of English experiences in the English of England, his language is bound to be related now to the English of America, or of Black Africa, or even of India. He may be personally committed or uncommitted, his spoken language is alive and sensitive to an increasingly single world.

It may be more difficult to discern how these general problems are reflected in music or painting. I think music is a somewhat special case because the polyphonic and harmonic music of the West is unlike anything that the rest of the world has ever heard before. It is so powerful and splendid a medium that all the rest of the world is learning it. If Europe exports musicians to other lands, they go to found academies and orchestras and opera houses, modelled on those of Europe. The jazz musicians go first (if only on discs) and the straight players eventually follow. There is a deceptive easiness about it, because the language of music (like the language of painting and sculpture) is without racial frontiers. But the danger to music is that this easiness of travel, combined with the lack of any rival musical tradition of equal power, can leave us Europeans distressingly complacent, stupidly unaware of the possibly parochial content of our art. We are apt to regard it as a merit in ourselves, when we restrict our view to, say, Salzburg or Bayreuth, for the past – or when we withdraw into the fortresses of coterie, for the present. To my mind such unawareness means a challenge evaded. This is not a choice and a sacrifice that I can commend to myself. I do not know what the objective consequences are to music, but I feel we have to live in the tension which awareness brings. Otherwise I am lacking in a certain quality of humanity.

It is much the same if we consider time rather than place. An endlessly increasing past demands from us an ever varying response. Malraux has gathered together into the acceptable image of the Imaginary Museum all this stimulus to contemporary artists in face of the accumulation of artefacts from bygone ages. I think the importance may be less in the practical possibility that individual artists can pick and choose their next style from the museum, if that is the way they work, than in the altered sense of history as a whole. If prototypes of one's pictures are preserved there in those caves from the Ice Age, then one's values are inescapably altered. Once again I feel that the apparent unaffectedness of music in this respect, owing to the impermanence of sound as a medium and our extreme preoccupation with the late-invented polyphony, is a deception. Drum, Pipe, and Zither (to use Yeats's title) have a history, one suspects, as old as paint. That men danced in the caves the very footprints will show us. But the rhythm and melodies to which they moved faded on the air at the instant. Yet with imagination, returning into the past through the music of living primitives, we can feel these rhythms in our blood, on our pulses now. And though that is not so sharp an experience as to see the picture preserved on the cave wall, it is of the same kind.

For myself, I ally this sense of the past with those Indian religious myths of creation which, unlike the story of a unique creation in Genesis, are designed to enforce the idea that creations and aeons have already been, and will be yet, innumerable. There is no rational means of bringing these contradictory apprehensions of time into unity, though they can both be savoured in the mind. There is a sense of Time as unique, from Genesis to World's End. And there is a sense of Time as repetitive, or circular – the myth of the Eternal Return. I am uncertain how objective is my feeling that the movement of these two ideas, one against the other, is another aspect of the new world picture; though others feel with me. I seem to want to think these ideas motionless, and so hope to consider dispassionately the choice and sacrifice that holding exclusively to one or the other involves. But no ideas are motionless, except to the intellect. As in all other aspects of the new world picture, we are challenged by a contradictory multiplicity of situations, to which we can only respond by choosing and by sacrificing.

The difficulty, and indeed the inadequacy, of such an elaborate rationalization of our predicaments as I have attempted to make here is, I hope, plain enough. It is indeed like commanding everything to be motionless so that the intellect can make a dispassionate judgement. But few things in life outside the realms of mathematical science (so far as that still remains certain) are thus motionless before the intellect: and art is not one of them – or at any rate only in a limited manner. There is always an aspect of art which throws the emphasis on measurement and relation, rather than on the sensuous. It is indeed possible so to exaggerate the idea of art as a once-for-all discovered system of relations that art can nearly disappear into mathematics. The tradition seems to come in the West from Pythagoras and through Plato. Some of the problems arising from it (viewed as a choice and a sacrifice) were lately discussed, in a perceptive article in *The Times Literary Supplement* concerning Mallarmé, not only in terms of poetry but by analogy with music and painting:

Since [such art's] true content is the perception of relations, it matters little in what order we perceive the things related: narrative sequences, temporal order and statement belong to the world of nature, time and chance. If things are truly in relationship, the relationship will emerge from every permutation of these things. Mallarmé intended to juggle with every possible combination of his elements of form as Bach juggled with incredibly varied arrangements of the elements of his theme in the Musical Offering. But in the most purely ingenious parts of the Musical Offering Bach's reversals and inversions of his theme were limited; he did not go in for purely mathematical permutations of notes.

Such perceptive writing helps us to set the claims of abstract art into proportion. We choose purity and we may sacrifice allure. We choose richness, and we may sacrifice form. Yet both these seemingly contradictory movements in art may spring from a response to the challenge of our time. The one may feel that only by setting the fundamental and unchanged purities of line and volume (to use sculptors' language) as an image before a debauched public can the creative artist be true to his function. The other may feel that only by enriching the sensibility in as many directions as possible ('Ripeness is all') can the starved soul of the technologist be given fresh nourishment to come alive again.

To sum up by reiterating one point: if our most real responsibilities are to inner values which are in opposition to the general run of our time, where do we get the strength to live by these values, as indeed we must, in all the societies that wish to make the expression of these values impossible? If, on the contrary, we live in a country where expression of these values is permitted, if discouraged, would it be peevish not to 'wear our tribulation like a rose'?

Part II

Preface to Poets in a Barren Age

In August 1971 I received a letter on B.B.C. paper from a young television director, Mischa Scorer, asking me if I would cooperate with him in a documentary film, in the series 'One Pair of Eyes'. It seems that sometime in his search for a suitable subject for the film he ran his hand along the book spines on his shelves and picked out a signed copy of the first edition of *Moving into Aquarius*. He re-read the book and then wrote me a carefully considered letter. What tempted me to accept was a sentence which began: 'For my part I can assure you of my desire to make a serious film . . .' I trustingly took the word 'serious' for truth not flummery. And the result – a rarity in television – was a very serious film indeed.

We found that as the cutting-room floor increasingly disappeared under feet of film, discarded in order to compress all into the 55 minutes allowed, the verbal complement became as increasingly vital and succinct. We could hardly waste a sentence. As a result the final text of what was spoken direct to camera or dubbed behind other film took on a precision and order which convinced the editor of *The Listener* that it should be published independent of the pictures.

In re-producing it now, there is a specific and a general point to be made.

Specifically the film did run for 55 minutes; but one reads the text in perhaps a half to a third of that time. So that, unlike reproduced radio talks, there is a constant discrepancy between the rate of presentation of the visual material as coordinated with the commentary and that of the printed text alone. The style suffers from being too fast and abrupt. Thus pictures of Jews being taken off to a Nazi concentration camp in a lorry to the singing of the spiritual 'Go down, Moses', leads in the film to a natural comment on why I used the five spirituals in *A Child of*

Our Time. Then the film cuts to howitzers being mounted in Horse Guards Parade, London. At which point the narrative is immediately and naturally concerned with war. But without the picture cut the text is unhappily abrupt.

Generally, of course, texts to film are incomplete without the pictures. The visual component, with the musical, affects us immediately and profoundly. The total experience of pictures, music and words is different from that of words alone. The reader must constantly bear in mind the original function of this piece, and take his bearings from the visual images which the references invoke. For the soldiers marching away to Flanders really did sing 'those songs'; the obscenities of Hiroshima and the death-camps appeared momentarily, unforgettably, before our eyes; Martin Luther King spoke his own words to thousands upon thousands facing the Lincoln Memorial in Washington D.C. and the organ pealed at his own funeral after the assassination; the moon rocket rose into the sky apparently out of the Albert Hall, London, as the Promenaders reached the thundering, comforting closing words of Parry's 'Jerusalem'.

Poets in a Barren Age

I am a composer. That is someone who imagines sounds, creating music from the inner world of the imagination. The ability to experience and communicate this inner world is a gift. Throughout history, society has recognized that certain men possess this gift and has accorded them a special place. But if such men – poets if you like – are honoured, are the products of their imagination of any real value to the society which honours them? Or are we, particularly at this present point in history, deluding ourselves that this may be so?

Like every creative artist, my days are spent pondering, considering, wrestling in my mind with an infinite permutation of possibilities. I must create order out of chaos. The act of imagination is sometimes of great intensity, sometimes more wayward and always, for a big piece of music, prolonged. I am, as it were, possessed, taken over by the creative drive from within, and even when I put away the manuscript paper I find it almost impossible to switch off the inner activity.

I have lived in the country since my student days. This is practical and personal. I need to shut myself away from the noise and activity of the town in order to find some kind of inner silence. The outside world with all its troubles goes on around my personal sanctuary, and I am fully aware of its harsh realities. And I face continually a question within this paradox: has the reality of my imagination any lasting relation to the reality of those events which immediately affect the lives of men? This is a question that has been asked by artists throughout history. And if we go back into history we begin to get some clues as to how society and the artist have seen each other.

A few miles from where I live is Avebury – one of the most fascinating and extraordinary relics of our distant past. It is a strange, strange place, full of magic, where certainly art and religion were practised together. It is four thousand years old, coming right out of our ancient past, and it's so enormous that it must have required a colossal feat of social organization to have raised those great stones into those circles. And it wasn't for things like defence or for living in: it was for practising ritual. Could we, by imagination, go back to that time, and see the people moving about, we would find that they danced to music and sang and dressed themselves in particular clothes, because at that time the religion and the art were absolutely together. Once we are inside this sort of sanctuary, we feel that the necessity, the drive, the instinct to make such a place where this kind of ritualistic art could occur, and where all the functions that we think art has are comprehended, is something so fundamental and deep-seated in human beings that there is no doubt that it must have existed always.

It is in prehistoric caves, such as those at Lascaux or Altamira, that we find the earliest examples of image-making. The artist who painted these animals fulfilled a definite function in his society, close to that of a priest or a magician. He painted not to excite the aesthetic feelings of his fellows, but to conjure the hunted animals into the net. For these Stone-Age people there was something supernatural and awe-inspiring about the very act of making an image. The Greeks were the first to name and define this mysterious act of artistic creation, and they called it 'divine madness'. Divine because in their metaphor it was inspired by the Gods; madness because it was uncontrollable by reason, like falling in love. The two concepts of beauty and goodness were felt to be so close together that one compound word was coined to express both. And because the artist was the creator of beauty, the Greeks gave him a dignity in their society unsurpassed in European history. With the rise of the first Europe of Catholic Christendom, value went over to the other world, to the spiritual. The artist's gifts were employed in teaching doctrine or in expressing the glory of God. And although his position in society was now that of an anonymous craftsman, he was still concerned with a profound mystery, with an attempt to express the in-expressible. He knew that the beauty of what he had made, whether it was a jewel or a cathedral, was a reflection of his maker.

By the end of the fifteenth century, the emphasis began to shift away from God and accrue to this world – the new, round world that had in it America and which was waiting to be explored. Man decided he could measure the heavens. This was the Renaissance, the gigantic turning-point of European history. Spiritual man gave way to anatomical man. Superstition – if that's the right word – gave place to science, and this at last led to the belief that human culture and progress are best obtained through technics. The result of this was that people came to feel that the world of imagination was secondary and inferior. In this new world – at least by the eighteenth century – the divinity of art was reduced to decoration and entertainment. In the elegant drawing-rooms and palaces, composers even of the genius of Haydn and Mozart created music for the diversion of a privileged minority. In so far as the artist was accepted he became the darling of the fashionable set, and for the first time in history began to think of himself as an artist with a capital 'A'.

This new self-consciousness, although implying a separation from the total fabric of society, was welcomed by the so-called 'Romantics' because it seemed to give them a very special value. It led them to believe that they, through Art, could set the world to rights. As Shelley claimed: 'Poets are the unacknowledged legislators of the world.' And think of Beethoven in his Ninth Symphony, exemplifying this arrogance, making confident assertions about the brotherhood of man: 'O ye millions, I embrace you. Fling this kiss to all the world!'

But what was happening outside while Beethoven wrote it, was something very different. Europe was being riven by the French Revolution and society turned upside down by the Industrial Revolution. It was indeed possible to feel that these artistic affirmations could be illusions and that the artist was right outside the realities of the social life of his period. And he was impotent – he neither conversed with God nor spoke realistically to his fellows. And this situation, this dilemma for the artist, has gone on virtually unchanged for a hundred and fifty years. It is the same now as it was for Beethoven. The feeling that the artist is excluded from the realities of his society, that what he wanted to speak of were things which his society found valueless and unreal. Hölderlin, a poet contemporary with Beethoven, mourning for his loss of function, raised the despairing cry: 'What are poets for in a barren age?' When I listen to someone else performing my music it is clear the music has left its creator and has a life of its own. But the nub of the question remains for me as it did for Hölderlin: 'What does this music – or any music – do within our present society, and what do I think I am doing by composing it?' Any answer, for me, must inevitably be tied up with my own life and the events I have lived through.

My generation was the same age as the century. I was born in 1905, lived in the depths of an unpolluted countryside and remained ignorant and innocent of all events outside the family until the start of the Great War. As the men marched away I remember the sense of their lighthearted confidence, singing those songs that gave me my first musical excitement. I was so young still that I could reduce the significance of the war to those songs. When the war ended, the springtime of my life coincided with the momentary springtime all Europe felt as the killing stopped. In 1923 I came to London as a student of eighteen. I now knew that my life lay in artistic creation. I had no misgivings whatsoever. I scarcely considered any of the great contemporary events which seemed to lie outside my musical needs, concerned only with the huge ferment of artistic creation of the period and the general mood – in England at any rate – of frenetic gaiety.

Into this nonchalant atmosphere there began to dawn the first truths about the war, and strangely enough this experience happened to me when I went to see the film *The Four Horsemen of the Apocalypse.* This was popular art. We all went to see Valentino in his latest movie. In fact I can recall nothing of the love story, all I remember is the violence and destruction of the war sequences. And what I never forgot was the extraordinary image of four horsemen flying across the screen at every moment of destruction, and the doom-laden sound of Beethoven's 'Coriolan' Overture. These things combined to give me the sense that there were enormous forces beyond human control which could simply destroy the whole fabric of our civilization. At the end of the film came the first pictures I had ever seen of the Flanders graveyards: row upon row of little white crosses. This gave me the horrified understanding that so many thousands of young men whom I had seen marching lightheartedly away, had ended under the earth. I burst into tears (virtually) and went out. I realized that although I was still a very young man and had a great deal to learn about the merely technical questions of music and was going to immerse myself in everything to do with the technique of my art, that this was something which I simply could not forget: there was a necessity for art of our time in some way, when it had learned its own techniques, to be concerned with what was happening to this 'apocalyptic' side of our present time.

What indeed was happening to all of us of my age in England, was a realization that the spring was false, and that in fact it was still winter. For the majority of my countrymen perhaps there had never been a spring at all. With this realization every artist of my generation became politically involved in some way or other. I remember how I went up North in 1932 to a work-camp, helping unemployed ironstone miners, then hiked into the coalfields and saw for the first time, with horrified eyes, the undernourished children. When I returned to the well-fed South, I was ashamed.

I saw now, and understood for the first time, the stark realities of human life for so many people and accepted the overwhelming need for compassion with regard to such things. So I was faced, consciously perhaps for the first time, with the fundamental question: had I the right to turn away from such reality, to shut myself up to write abstract music? I could have said music is something so disrelated to this reality that everybody must go out and take political or philanthropic action in order to have some immediate impact upon the situation. Every artist was faced with this at that time as they have perhaps always been. It was a real dilemma and it was not solved by a moral determination to know which was which, but by the fact that the actual drive of one's needs as an artist was so great that it forced me back to the studio for the purpose of writing music, although I was quite certain somewhere that at some point, music could have a direct relation also to the compassion that was so deep in my own heart.

There were other huge political forces on the boil. Not only socialism but fascism. With the meteoric rise of Hitler, a kind of mad irrationality appeared in Europe, so truly evil that few of us had any experience to understand it. The whole Jewish race was to be systematically liquidated it appeared.

Although the artist appears to be locked away, doing his particular thing, one could not, at that time, but be aware of what was going on. I was almost peculiarly aware. I was drawn by something of my own entrails into what was happening, particularly in Germany. The Jews were the particular scapegoats of everything, for every kind of standing outcast, whether in Russia or America or even in England. For these people I knew somehow I had to sing songs. Suddenly, in fact the day after war broke out, the whole thing welled up in me in a way which I can remember exactly. I simply had to go and begin to write *A Child of Our Time*. I felt I had to express collective feelings and that could only be done by collective tunes such as the Negro spirituals, for these tunes contain a deposit of generations of common experience.

As the preparations for war began in earnest, I watched but did not take part. I knew that something was forcing me to be a Conscientious Objector. For failing to carry out my conditions of exemption I was given a prison sentence and was locked away in Wormwood Scrubbs. I was now myself an outcast. It seemed indeed that this particular split between myself and society was part of the continuous and wider split between the artist affirming what he believes to be absolute values, and society which seemed bent on destroying itself. The climax of my sense of isolation came shortly afterwards when the noble Christian allies decided to put their faith in that masterpiece of technics – the atom bomb. Simultaneously, the concentration camps were opened. I found in these obscenities, as did many others, a most violent and enduring shock to my sense of what humanity might be at all. A denial of any and every affirmation which the poet might make, whether in the name of God or of Mankind. What price Beethoven now?

Whenever I come back to the places where the great seas meet the primeval granite, I am curiously refreshed. Because as I look I get the sense that it's been there long before human beings, and that it has been made under the fantastic pressures of the cooling earth and the sea which is totally destructive of anything that comes in its way. And even further, if we look around at all that has happened to us as human beings, we feel that we too are susceptible to just the same chaos, the same violence, the same unpredictability, the same kind of impersonal passion of irrational forces, that make a mockery of all our idealistic and rationalistic intentions. But, however much we may be aware of the chaotic forces we also have the opposite within us, the complementary need for harmony and goodness. Deep within me, I know that part of the artist's job is to renew our sense of the comely and the beautiful. To create a dream. Every human being has this need to dream. It might seem that this need is satisfied by the simplicities of popular art but behind the mass demand for entertainment lies somewhere the desire for something more permanent, for the deeper satisfaction of proportion and beauty in a world of impersonal exploitation – a world which has no care for the inner person. And if for the poet this means a barren age what does he mean by 'barren'? Our age is not technologically barren. Technology means power and vast production through machines. So man can apparently accomplish everything for good or ill. He can produce abundance, he can manufacture milk powder for starving children in vast quantities. Technology has potentially all the answers for a hungry world.

The barrenness of the age lies in the deprivation of man's imaginative life once he has put all value into machines. As man becomes more and more capable scientifically, the debasement of the world of imagination produces human beings who find it harder to use decently the material abundance thus provided.

Technology has produced such huge extensions to our means of communication that as we look at photos of the starving and the dead of Bangladesh we are moved – through newspapers and television we are moved more often and more widely. Although we cannot accept that all men really will be brothers we perhaps know more about what being brothers means, because we have seen and understood the opposite. We are acutely aware of what it means to be human.

When I look at the exuberance of young people today I see the paradox between the precision and accuracy and power of the scientific world and the primitive, uncouth, even psychedelic nature of the world of popular art at its sharpest. I think the universality of this psychedelic craving is a symptom of an acutely felt imbalance in our society, an imbalance which denies the needs of the impoverished raw world of the inner self.

There are other dreams – apparently political, often incoherent. As in my youth, it is the prerogative of young men to shout for a better world. The outstanding feature of this unrest today is its universality. The outbreaks of student protest all over the world have perhaps less to do with any specific political issues than with a widespread impatience with a society that appears to have little time for dreams.

Martin Luther King said: 'I have a dream. I have a dream that my four little children will one day live in a nation where they will not be judged by the colour of their skin but by the content of their character.'

The dream is broken, as it is time and time again. The dream of the French Revolution, of the British Empire, of the 'War to end War', of the communist's Utopia. Most resounding of all for our time – Jefferson's dream of an America which accepts that all men are created equal. That dream is broken. But must I stop singing, like Hölderlin, because of the fragility of all aspiration? I do not think this is what happens. We celebrate – even in outdated forms at time, because we must. The young people who sing that great hymn of affirmation, Blake's 'Jerusalem', are not so naïve as to imagine that they will in fact build it any more than that all mankind will be brothers. Yet there is a momentary vision of a possibility. The illusion we have now to discard is that this Jerusalem is still to be found outside, somewhere among the glittering promises of technology. As they leave the earth, the astronauts see it from afar – flat, round, nothing so small as a man to be seen. And that flattened out picture of the earth has always seemed to me to symbolize the devaluation of the singular, minute, particular man we all are. But I am still me on the earth and the astronaut is still one particular man on his moon. And it's my task as an artist to talk to him, to find some way to speak through the space suit of the technological man to the imaginative man within.

If art in our time seems to be standing on its head, taking on peculiar and even perverse forms, screaming in order to get attention, it's because it has been searching for the new languages we need if we are to speak to the millions of the modern world. It seems as though we've come to a point in our long history where value is returning to the world within.

Our faith in progress through technics is less absolute and because the hunger for this inner world is so alive in all of us and because this is the world the artist speaks immediately to, for the first time since the Renaissance it seems the time may be coming when the artist is once more at one with his society.

I have been writing music for forty years. During those years there have been huge and world-shattering events in which I have been inevitably caught up. Whether society has felt music valuable or needful I have gone on writing because I must. And I know that my true function within a society which embraces all of us, is to continue an age-old tradition, fundamental to our civilization, which goes back into pre-history and will go forward into the unknown future. This tradition is to create images from the depths of the imagination and to give them form whether visual, intellectual or musical. For it is only through images that the inner world communicates at all. Images of the past, shapes of the future. Images of vigour for a decadent period, images of calm for one too violent. Images of reconciliation for worlds torn by division. And in an age of mediocrity and shattered dreams, images of abounding, generous, exuberant beauty.*

*These last four sentences were deliberately quoted almost verbatim from the end of chapter 9 in Part 1. Despite the presently suspect word 'beauty', I felt I could not express the matter better.

Preface to Verses for a Symphony

In 1965 I was listening to some contemporary music at a concert at Edinburgh when I realized that my mind had ceased to attend, as it had previously, to events in the concert hall and had entered its own interior world of conception and creation. That is to say, while I heard the music in the hall still proceeding, I began to perceive possibilities for music of my own. This is not an unusual experience for a creative personality. In my own case I don't hear any exact musical phrases with this interior ear, but the music outside constructs a kind of protective shell, which the inner creative activity seems to favour.

When I compose at the piano I produce this protective shell myself by surrounding my ears with a piano approximation of, say, the orchestral or vocal score I am working on. Here the external shell and the interior imaginative activity are seemingly congruous. When a conception or an idea springs unbidden into the mind during a concert (or, as sometimes happens to me, when sounds in nature, e.g. wind on big trees in leaf, make the protective shell), the interior musical imagination creates only momentarily and in very broad sweeps. At the Edinburgh concert I turned to my neighbour, Karl Hawker, I remember, and said, 'The Third Symphony has begun'.

There followed the usual years of prolonged but only occasional formulation and consideration, while other compositions were being written, and the Symphony itself did not reach the desk until the spring of 1970. And by that time also I had written the text of the four songs which were to be part of the finale.

I have learned to become my own librettist mainly for two reasons. First, I know what I want to say and am prepared to work hard to achieve some reasonable verbal metaphor. Second, there usually are musical considerations which impinge on the verbal. (As someone recently said about the Beatles, 'Their unique quality was to know at which points a scrap of ordinary language needed to be touched in order to make it sing.') Thus the first three of these four songs are blues or blues-derived: slow, fast, slow. The verses, invariably strophic, had to have the appropriate number of words. And since the first song is a deliberately simple, almost classic approach to my own style of blues, the verse has the primitive early blues structure of AAB strophes. But in the dramatic scena of the fourth song, I needed to refer musically and verbally to Schiller's *Ode to Joy* as sung by the chorus in Beethoven's Ninth Symphony. So the German couplet

> Alle Menschen werden Brüder
> Wo dein sanfter Flügel weilt

becomes transmuted into

> They sang that when she braved her wings
> The Goddess Joy would make us one.

While a little later, for the purposes of dramatization, I permitted myself a burst of, what I afterwards called, Nobodaddy-rhetoric (impermissible to any true poet!) preceding some dream of the Peaceable Kingdom.

Since the fourth song refers thus specifically to the grandiose affirmations of Schiller's *Ode to Joy*, so confidently addressed to the millions of the world, it had seemed to me that Schiller might be considered the songs' originator. But, as Colin Davis pointed out when he first read the verses, the true exemplar is Schiller's contemporary, Blake. These are songs of innocence and experience: two and two. They pose the same fundamental, unanswerable questions about the universe and man's destiny, though their language cannot emulate Blake's incomparable verse.

To his period's belief in natural law (the belief, which underpins Jefferson's magnificent opening to the American Declaration of Independence of 1776) Blake asked: What true law of equity can be found in a nature that has produced both the Tyger and the Lamb? (Or as he put it once in an aphorism: 'One Law for the Lion and Ox is Oppression.') Again, to those who still held to the Christian creed, he cried: How can you believe both in

Nobodaddy-Jehovah who demanded 1,000 Amalekite foreskins as a sacrifice, and an all-forgiving Jesus? The answer in our own day is that we cannot. It is better for us to accept the Tyger and the Lamb, Jehovah and Jesus, as enduring states of our common humanity ('My sibling was the torturer'), now one, now the other in the ascendant.

What is 'out-of-date' in Schiller's concept of joy is any romantic notion of its universality and inevitability. All that has happened since, in aid of various political utopias, has but deepened the disillusion. Yet if now is our Season in Hell, then when we occasionally celebrate, as we must and if we can, we do so from a deeper need and with a sharper pang.

Verses for a Symphony

I

As I drew nurture from my mother's breast
As I drew nurture from my mother's breast
I drank in sorrow with her milk.

As I stood upright on my father's knee
As I stood upright on my father's knee
I drank in sorrow with his kiss.

Blood of their blood
Bone of their bone
What then is me that was not them?

II

O, I'll go walking with my nostrils
quivering and my eyeballs
flashing and my mouth
round open laughing and my tongue,
My tongue on fire.

O, I'll go whirling with my armpits
glist'ning and my breast-buds
shaking and that navel,
which my mother left me,
luxuriously dreaming.

O, I'll go prancing with my toe-tips
flying and my knee-bones
jerking and my thighs,
with what between there lies,
My thighs aflame.

III

I found the man grown to a dwarf.
After the circus, in his tent, he said:
So many take me for a doll.
    I gave him milk and kisses.

I found the girl born dumb and blind.
She stroked my hand and tap-wrote in the palm:
I feel but cannot see the sun.
    I gave her milk and kisses.

I found the beautiful moronic child.
His smiling eyes shone bright; he said:
Nothing; for his mind is lost.
    I gave him milk and kisses.

As I lay down beside my mate,
Body to body,
We did not heed the sorrow.

Ah merciful God, if such there be,
Let him, let her, be born straight.
But if no answer to the prayer,
    We *shall* give milk
    We *shall* give kisses.

IV

They sang that when she waved her wings,
The Goddess Joy would make us one.

And did my brother die of frostbite in the camp?
And was my sister charred to cinders in the oven?

We know not so much joy
For so much sorrow –
Though my fine body dances;
Nor so much evil –
Though I sometimes be good.
My sibling was the torturer.
He takes his place.

So if the worm was given love-lust,
Let him stay patient in his place.
But if the cherub stands b'fore God,
Let him demote himself to man,
Then spit his curses across the celestial face
Though he be answered (Answered!?)
With annihilation from the whirlwind.

It is our agony
We fractured men
Surmise a deeper mercy;
That no god has shown.

I have a dream
That my strong hand shall grip the cruel
That my strong mouth shall kiss the fearful
That my strong arms shall lift the lame
And on my giant legs we'll whirl our way
Over the visionary earth
In mutual celebration.

What though the dream crack!
We shall remake it.
Staring with those startled eyes at what we are –
Blood of my blood
Bone of my bone
We sense a huge compassionate power
To heal
To love.

Postscript

For some time I carried around in my wallet a cutting from *The Times Literary Supplement* of a review of the publication of Brecht's play *Die Ermittlung*. The cutting, however, has no date and the review, in T.L.S. tradition, is anonymous. The relevant portion reads:

One episode, however, goes to the heart of the problem. A witness tells of a Gestapo man who was preparing his A-levels. Leaving the famous ramp on which men and women were selected for the ovens and small children trodden to a pulp, Stark invites a number of the more educated inmates to a study session. They are to help him review his reading and to hear him present a paper on 'Humanism in Goethe'. This is where a play about Auschwitz might one day start. It would show Herr Stark reading a very good paper and passing his *Staatsexamen* with merit. It would follow his career as university graduate, teacher of literature, and father of handsome, well-behaved children. It would show him educating others, a mere ten or fifteen years later, to a love of Goethe, as expert and sincere as his own. *Goethe at Auschwitz* (or *Mozart at Belsen*, or *Shakespeare on l'où veut*). This is the juxtaposition that remains most frightening, that calls loudest for insight. Only the great artist can give it and thereby reaffirm the role of the imagination against the dead veracity of the fact.

I kept this cutting close, not so much for the perceptions of its aesthetics, but as a constant corrective to my natural pride in the three great masters of the imagination named within it. That is to say, a corrective, not to the pride in what these creative minds and bodies had achieved, but to any lingering belief that humanist art could achieve that moral power over and within humanity which religious art, and, indeed, traditional religion itself had failed to engender.

The religious failure is perhaps the simpler to define. Not simpler to solve, of course, but at least sharper to present. Let us begin with the Jews in the camps. Some of them may have kept the faith and practised the righteousness of their forefathers, Shadrag, Mischak and Abednego, yet they knew as a fact that no angel of Jehovah would uphold them unscathed in the ovens when their time came. Something had happened to the relation between the chosen people and their God since the earlier event. And has not something happened also to the relationship of the chosen people to the unchosen?

Superficially the faithful Christian might be thought to be in better religious heart. He, after all, would be eternally in heaven, while his torturer (even though a Christian believer himself, at least on Sundays) would be eternally in hell (traditionally a more prolonged oven) unless he managed to repent before death. But no Christian in Belsen or Auschwitz believed like that, however realistically his Christian precursors had believed in that fashion at their martyrdom or fiery purification at the sectarian stake. Not only is there now no longer any miracle of divine intervention at the request of private prayer, even if accompanied by the most steadfast faith and exemplary righteousness, but there is also no true Christian satisfaction any more to be drawn from the pleasure of divine reward as the price of divine retribution. Though I am not myself a believer I can state this so bluntly because it forms the present core of Christian anxiety and the strange fount of Christian compassion: let us try at least to make up for the failure of God's mercy!

The same inability to achieve moral authority is to be found even in so-called secular religions. If the Marxist believer, for example, had the illusion that communist idealism would somehow extract him from the slave-labour of the work-camps (let alone from the interrogation in the prisons) he was equally mistaken. There is no hope for a resolution of the ethical or religious problem here. (Nor can the artist, be he even Solzhenitsyn, produce a resolution – though a catharsis perhaps.)

And does Hiroshima, where so many thousands were radioactively incinerated in a flash, belong in this grim inquiry? Certainly, to the extent it has pin-pointed the ethical ambivalence of a supposedly neutral, rational, empirical, pure science. But that event, which shook the world for a time more agonizingly than concentration camp or work-camp obscenities, made its greatest impact through its threat to our survival. Once the balance of deterrence was seen to work, the ethical disturbance, which had been conjoined with survival fears, fell away as the fears receded. At least, that is to say, it fell out of the head-lines, though never out of the totality of the problem.

Part of the process which underlies and leads to *all* these horrors is the holier-than-thou syndrome: whether of the chosen of God; of the biologically chosen Aryan race; of the ideologically chosen orthodox party member; or of whatever and whatever. Implied in every acceptance of the chosen is the acceptance, as a complementary fact, of the rejected. If we are righteous, they are evil; if we are revolutionary heroes, they are reactionary scum; if we are human, they are sub-human. To make the world pure for us, they shall be exterminated. The ends justify the means.

Alas they do not. Or perhaps, mercifully they do not. Someone once said: every secret police is counter-revolutionary. Brutalities can only be performed by brutes (if brutes for a season), bestialities by beasts (if beasts for a season). The Nazi regime went down in a horrible war, and to that extent the season was over. It is a graver problem where the K.G.B. (or equivalent) has been in season for fifty years until it permeates society like a cancer; inoperable but never terminal. Is the K.G.B. interrogator a monster produced by this cancer, or just a worthy executioner smudging out the good society's anti-social refuse?

Which brings me to the observation that we have massive documentary accounts from persons who have survived the obscenities, but virtually no confessional documentation from anyone who has committed them, whether in his season brute, beast, or self-righteous hero.

To return to the more metaphysical matters. If we cannot make God, that is to say our particular 'local' righteousness, any longer an alibi for the brutalities we use against an alien righteousness; and if no received religion or ideology that we know can dispense with the claim to exclusivity of such righteousness, then our state might seem desperate. The way forward may seem like universal anarchy and despair. But as Blake – that maverick of the eighteenth century – once put it:

> If the Sun and Moon should doubt,
> They'd immediately Go out.

Since the Sun and Moon do not Go out, this notion of absolute doubt is clearly not a built-in function of the universe. How indeed could it be? And since in Blake's metaphorical language Sun, Moon and all the Stars are encompassed within humanity's imagination and desire, then *total* doubt (in the sense of *universal* suicide) is not a built-in function of the human condition either. The absolute (and the camps showed this over and over again, when people laughed, joked, made love and even fell deeply in love, during the disgusting struggle for survival) is that humanity *cannot* go out; it *must* go on. And imagination and desire nourish our ever-renewed hope.

But imagination and desire are strange, terrible, poetic words. And indeed, *Who* sings? *Who* dreams?

> Be not afeard; the isle is full of noises,
> Sounds and sweet airs, that give delight, and hurt not.
> Sometimes a thousand twangling instruments
> Will hum about mine ears; and sometimes voices,
> That, if I then had waked after long sleep,
> Will make me sleep again; and then, in dreaming,
> The clouds, methought, would open and show riches
> Ready to drop upon me: that, when I waked,
> I cried to dream again.

That was not sung by Ariel, but by Caliban ('thou earth, thou') out of his darkness. From the same rich vein of dreams I have quarried a short quotation from an early letter of Jung's, which I have composed into a couplet in a new libretto.

> Take care for the earth.
> God will take care for himself.

In the Introduction to this book in its first edition, I made what seemed to me then a long-overdue acknowledgment to Jung. But once that earlier period of preoccupation with Jung's ideas had ceased, I experienced, as I have so often done in such cases, the greatest reluctance ever to return to his writings. Recently, however, I heard over the radio some readings from the English translation of his collected letters. There were portions of letters concerning life and death, so profoundly moving and wise, that I decided to buy the new publication. So, as it were, I come full circle. Here (but not one of the passages I found so moving) is the relevant substance of a letter of 1929.

We live in the age of the decline of Christianity, when the meta-physical premises of morality are collapsing. (Recently I saw Wells at my house, who said the same thing, and rubbed his nose with his finger, which meant: Then we ought to know – or smell – what we can do now.) That's why the young are experimenting like young dogs. They want to live experimentally, with no historical premises. That causes reactions in the unconscious, restlessness, and longing for the fulfilment of the times. (This is called 'Chiliasm'). When the confusion is at its height a new revelation comes, i.e. at the beginning of the 4th month of world history.

That is, at the year 2000 AD the 2,000-year world 'month' of Pisces – shall we say, of ideological purity and fratricide – goes over gradually into the 'month' of Aquarius – shall we say, of compassion and attempted union of the opposites.

This follows psychological rules. . . . People like you must *look* at everything and *think* about it and communicate with the heaven that dwells deep within them and listen inwardly for a word to come. At the same time organize your outward life properly so that your voice carries weight.*

That would surely be 'moving into Aquarius' with dignity and power.

* *C. G. Jung's Letters*, vol. 1, Routledge & Kegan Paul, 1973.

Index

HISTORY

ANATOMY OF THE SS STATE   Helmut Krausnick & Martin Broszat   60p

The inside story of the concentration camps, 'probably the most impressive work on the Nazi period ever to appear' *TES*.

ART AND THE INDUSTRIAL REVOLUTION
Francis D. Klingender   (*illustrated*)   75p

One of the most original and arresting accounts of the impact of the new industry and technology upon the landscape of England and the English mind. 'There is no book like it.' *John Betjeman*.

ASPECTS OF THE FRENCH REVOLUTION
Alfred Cobban   75p

The origins of the Revolution, the role of the Enlightenment, *The Parlement*, the diamond necklace affair. 'A tremendous and enviable achievement of scholarship.' *David Thomson*.

THE BORGIAS   Michael Mallet   (*illustrated*)   90p

The rise and fall of one of the most notorious families in European history: Legends of poisoning, incest, and political contrivance.

CONSCIOUSNESS AND SOCIETY   H. Stuart Hughes   75p

The re-orientation of European social thought from 1890–1930; the ideas and works of Freud, Croce, Bergson, Jung, Sorel, Weber, Durkheim, Proust, Mann, Gide, Hesse, etc.

THE DEATH OF LORCA   Ian Gibson   (*illustrated*)   £1·00

Frederico Garcia Lorca, one of the outstanding poets and dramatists of this century, was murdered by Nationalist rebels at the outbreak of the Spanish Civil War in 1936. History enshrines him as a homosexual romantic martyr, but his political convictions are indisputable. 'Lovers of poetry, lovers of truth, lovers of Spain should all read this exemplary piece of literary research.'
The Sunday Times.

HISTORY – *contd.*

THE MONKS OF WAR Desmond Seward (*illustrated*) £1·00

The courageous and often savagely brutal history of the military religious orders; a compulsive epic of the Knights Templar, the hospitallers and the Teutonic Knights.

THE MYTHOLOGY OF THE SECRET SOCIETIES
J. M. Roberts £1·50

A spectre haunted 18th and 19th century European history; that a secret society would seize power. It was a false myth. 'J. M. Roberts has written an important and scholarly essay on the conspiracy theory of history.' *Sunday Telegraph*

A NEW HISTORY OF THE UNITED STATES
William Miller 6op

A brilliant exposition of the events and ideas which have shaped American history, from the early Renaissance voyages of exploration to the beginning of the Space Age.

THE PURSUIT OF THE MILLENNIUM
Norman Cohn (*illustrated*) 75p

Revolutionary millenarians and mystical anarchists in the Middle Ages roamed Europe searching for redemption. A masterpiece of the history of ideas.

THE QUEST FOR ARTHUR'S BRITAIN
Geoffrey Ashe (*illustrated*) £1·00

The story of Arthur and the Knights of the Round Table, the chief myth of Britain. How true is it?

RUSSIA IN REVOLUTION Lionel Kochan £1·00

A compact, readable and authoritative account of one of the most important events in modern history.

ARTS

ART AND THE INDUSTRIAL REVOLUTION
Francis D. Klingender   (*illustrated*)   75p

One of the most original and arresting accounts of the impact of
the new industry and technology upon the landscape of England
and the English mind. 'There is no book like it.' *John Betjeman.*

AWOPBOPALOOBOP ALOPBAMBOOM   Nik Cohn
(*illustrated*)   50p

The original ultimate celebration of rock music: Pop from the
beginning.

THE CITIZEN KANE BOOK
Pauline Kael, Orson Welles, Herman Mankiewicz   (*illustrated*)
£1·25
The complete shooting script and story behind one of the greatest
films ever made.

DESIGN FOR THE REAL WORLD
Victor Papanek   (*illustrated*)   90p

A revolutionary re-appraisal of the role of design, possibly the most
important manifesto since the Bauhaus.

THE FILMGOER'S COMPANION   Leslie Halliwell   £1·50

The world's most comprehensive, compact and lauded
encyclopaedia of cinema and cinema folk. Over 7,000 entries.

FOLK SONG IN ENGLAND   A. L. Lloyd   £1·50

The classic history of the natural expressions of the British people.

THE HIDDEN ORDER OF ART
Anton Ehrenzweig   (*illustrated*)   75p

A brilliant enquiry into the psychology of artistic creativity,
ranging from the music of Mozart and Cage to the paintings of
Michelangelo and Raschenberg.

ARTS – *contd.*

MYTHOLOGIES   Roland Barthes   50p

An entertaining and elating introduction to the science of
semiology – the study of the signs and signals through which
society expresses itself, from the leading intellectual star.

THE SOCIOLOGY OF ART   Jean Duvignaud   40p

An examination of the underlying influences of painting by a leading
French critic.

THE SORROW AND THE PITY   Marcel Ophuls   £1·00

The chronicle of a French city under the German occupation, the
text and illustrations from the film.

THE VOICES OF SILENCE   Andre Malraux   £1·90

The ultimate exposition of all art from prehistory to modern
photography and cinema: The museum without walls.
600 illustrations.

All these books are available at your local bookshop or newsagent; or can be
ordered direct from the publisher. Just tick the titles you want and fill in the
form below.

Name...

Address ....

....

Write to Paladin Cash Sales, P.O. Box 11, Falmouth, Cornwall TR10 9EN.
Please enclose remittance to the value of the cover price plus 10p postage
and packing for one book, 5p for each additional copy.
Granada Publishing reserve the right to show new retail prices on covers,
which may differ from those previously advertised in the text or elsewhere.